THE
HAWAI'I
TAILGATE
COOKBOOK

Grilling Recipes From
Top Island Chefs

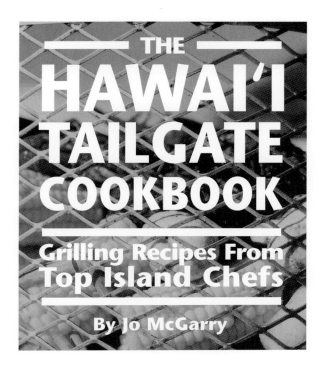

THE HAWAI'I TAILGATE COOKBOOK

Grilling Recipes From Top Island Chefs

By Jo McGarry

WATERMARK
PUBLISHING

© 2004 by Watermark Publishing
All rights reserved. No part of this book may be reproduced in
any form or by any electronic or mechanical means, including
information retrieval systems, without prior written permission
from the publisher, except for brief passages quoted in reviews.

Copyright ownership of photographs and
recipes is retained by individual contributors.

ISBN 0-9742672-9-5

Library of Congress Control Number: 2004109632

Design
Leo Gonzalez

Production
Julie Chun

Photos by Jo McGarry, Lori Daniels and Brett Uprichard
(pp. 48, 64) or provided by individual chefs. Back cover photo
by Ronen Zilberman.

Watermark Publishing
1088 Bishop Street, Suite 310
Honolulu, HI 96813
Telephone: Toll-free 1-866-900-BOOK
Web site: www.bookshawaii.net
email: sales@bookshawaii.net

Printed in the Republic of Korea

Contents

Acknowledgments

When you're compiling a book that's basically a collection of other people's ideas and inspiration, you naturally want to thank everyone involved. A cookbook like this just isn't possible without the willingness of Hawai'i's chefs to share their secrets and participate in community projects. To all chefs, I extend my sincerest thanks. I look forward to continuing to work with you all in the coming years.

Thank you also to Margie Yoshioka, Don Murphy and the crew at Gaspro, not only for sharing their recipes and grilling techniques, but also for sharing tailgates with me and the hundreds of people who've been our guests over the years.

And to Betty Shimabukuro, who took on the task of editing and organizing these recipes—no mean feat, believe me; to Lori Daniels, who shared her tailgating photos; and to Jim Webb, whom we think of every time we hear the blender roar.

And finally, my thanks to everyone who takes the time to get to Aloha Stadium early on a Saturday afternoon and set up some of the best tailgates in the country. To those of you who shared your family recipes—mahalo! And to those who tune in to KKEA 1420 AM on your way to the stadium to hear the weird and wonderful tailgate parties that we find, I thank you all for listening. It just wouldn't be the same without you.

Aloha,
Jo McGarry

Introduction

As part of my job as restaurant specialist for *The Honolulu Star-Bulletin* and food columnist for *MidWeek*, I'm required to eat out. A lot. I also need to know what's happening on the local food scene and when change is in the air. Having eaten pigs' ears and tasted mountain oysters, among other local delicacies, I thought I'd done pretty well assimilating myself into the culture. After moving to Hawai'i from Scotland, I learned the secret to making good kim chee and was even able to order a shave ice correctly at Waiola Store. But there was one thing I'd missed out on. I didn't even realize it until 1998, when KCCN, the radio station that aired my daily talk show, asked me to host *The Tailgate Show*.

Veteran broadcaster Don Robbs explained the deal. The show had employed a number of hosts over its ten-year run, and now it needed someone to bring something a little, well, different to the table. My first afternoon on the local tailgate scene was something I will always remember.

There's something about that char-grilled smell, the sweetness of well-marinated teriyaki chicken and smoke rising from a steak as it starts to sizzle, that really makes me appreciate great food. This is even more true when you multiply it by 10,000 people at Aloha Stadium. I loved island tailgating from my very first report. Now I can't wait until August rolls around each year, so I can check out what's happening on the local grills.

Tailgating in Hawai'i has reached an unprecedented level of sophistication. That might be plain grilled fish on a simple hibachi, but take a closer look: There's a good chance that the fire is kiawe wood and the fish was fresh-caught this morning, off a local reef.

We love to tailgate in Hawai'i. We have the weather, of course, but more than that, we have history. Many groups of tailgaters have been cooking and eating together for 20 years or more and reunite at the beginning of football season like long-lost family. We also have truly wonderful ingredients: Fresh fish, Island-grown pork and beef, ala'e salt and wonderful produce—all essential elements of a great tailgate.

And we have incredible chefs. Not just the well-known ones you'll find in these pages, but enthusiastic and devoted hobbyists who put together incredible meals for their family and friends, lovingly cooking their creations over open-air grills.

I know about these folks because I meet them every football season in the Aloha Stadium parking lot. I know their stories, their devotion to University of Hawai'i football, and their love of food eaten in the great outdoors. So—those of you who marinate pigs' ears, make your own kim chee and catch your own opelu; those who bring white tablecloths and fine wines to the stadium because you enjoy making a good thing better; and those who just love the fact that you can wear shorts and drink beer in a parking lot in December—this book is for you.

Happy eating!

MY FIRST TAILGATE

They say that fools rush in…and in 1998, I was asked to host *The Tailgate Show*, KCCN 1420 AM's long-running pre-game show that airs an hour before each home game. I thought it sounded like lots of fun, although I had never been to a tailgate in my life. The day before the UH opener, I was interviewed on KCCN by the host of the station's morning sports talk show, Bobby Curran. I remember saying to him, "I just don't get why people want to drive to a parking lot, open their trunks, and then start cooking." Remember, now, I come from Scotland, where the weather prohibits just about any outdoor activity.

Bobby was gracious in his response, but I remember him telling me later he was thinking, "They've got this girl who's never been to a tailgate party hosting the show?" Everyone was waiting to see what would happen. I don't think I admitted to anyone (including him) that I'd never even seen a football game.

I also remember calling my friends in Edinburgh the night before the game and explaining to them that I was going to be doing live radio reports from "a parking lot where people eat hot dogs."

Sometimes it's better not to know too much. The program was a great success, and I began a love affair with tailgating that has grown with each passing year. My knowledge of football is fairly good now, too. I understand what's happening at the tailgates, and on the turf.

I don't know if I owe that to dedication, though—or to the fact that I married the sportscaster who couldn't believe I'd never been to a tailgate.

Ryan Day

Ryan Day is the executive chef at the Plantation Café, the Ala Moana Hotel's signature restaurant. I really enjoy his style of cooking—he calls it "American bistro cuisine"—which showcases the best of local products, using fresh herbs, greens and produce.

But he's a Southern boy at heart, and he's never happier than when he's wielding some barbecue tongs and holding open the grill top. He's just about the most enthusiastic chef to join our band of tailgaters, and his recipes remind me of those old Carolina barbecue joints. "I love to tailgate," he says. "When I was first starting out, I learned everything from cooking great ribs to making pulled pork sandwiches. I love to get the chance to cook anything on the barbecue."

At the Plantation Café, Ryan oversees a number of eagerly awaited annual food festivals, including Oktoberfest, a Tempura Fest and, most recently, a Swiss Fest (joined by veteran chef Martin Wyss). And on weekends, wherever you find Ryan tailgating, you'll find the Ala Moana Hotel's Director of Food and Beverage, Keith Koehler, close by. They make a great team—two great guys who know the meaning of the word "fun" when it comes to good food.

Australian Summer Lamb Rack with Shiraz Reduction

1	rack of lamb, trimmed of visible fat

Marinade

2 tbsp.	olive oil
2 cloves	garlic, peeled and crushed
1 sprig	rosemary, crushed
1 sprig	thyme, crushed
1 sprig	oregano, crushed

Sauce

1/2 bottle	Rosemount Shiraz
1 tbsp.	minced garlic
2 tbsp.	black peppercorns
2 tbsp.	cornstarch
1/2 cup	demi-glace

Marinate lamb in oil, garlic and herbs in the refrigerator overnight. Preheat oven to 400 degrees. Drain and dry lamb rack. Heat sauté pan and sear lamb on all sides. Roast in oven to preferred doneness, about 20 minutes or until it reaches 140 degrees on a meat thermometer. Remove from oven and let rest 10 minutes. Slice between bones. To make sauce: Combine Shiraz, minced garlic and peppercorns in a pot and bring to a half-simmer. Cook until wine is reduced by half. Add cold water to cornstarch to make a slurry of a syrupy consistency. Whisk slurry and demi-glace into wine sauce and simmer until syrupy.

Serves 2-3

Mandarin Chicken Salad

1-1/2 cups	mesclun greens
1 cup	Sweet Chili Dressing
1/4 cup	toasted pine nuts
1/2 cup	mandarin orange segments
1/2 cup	sliced cucumbers
2	6-oz. chicken breasts, grilled and sliced
1/2 cup	bean sprouts

Sweet Chili Dressing

32-oz. bottle	sweet chili sauce
1/2 cup	red wine vinegar
2 tbsp.	minced garlic
2 tbsp.	minced ginger
1 cup	olive oil
	salt and pepper, to taste

To make dressing: Mix sweet chili sauce with ginger, garlic and vinegar. Slowly whisk in olive oil. Add salt and pepper to taste. Makes 1 quart. (This recipe will make more dressing than you'll need, but it's good to have on hand. Store any extra in the refrigerator.) Toss salad greens in dressing, and fan chicken pieces out over them. Garnish with nuts, orange slices, cucumber and sprouts.

Serves 2

Chicken-Fried Steak

4	tenderized beef cutlets (known in supermarkets as "cube steak"), about 6 oz. each
1	egg
1 cup	milk
1-1/2 cups	flour
1/2 tsp.	salt
1/4 tsp.	paprika
1/4 tsp.	ground black pepper
1/4 tsp.	white pepper
1 cup	melted shortening or vegetable oil

Cream Gravy

3/4 cup	milk
3/4 cup	water
	flour, as needed

Beat egg and milk together; set aside. Mix flour and spices in a plate. Dip each cutlet in milk/egg mixture, dredge in flour mixture, and then dip back into milk/egg mixture. Save any leftover flour mixture. Pour shortening or oil, about 1/2-inch deep, into a large heavy skillet. Heat over medium-high heat for a few minutes until a drop of egg/milk mixture added to the oil pops and sizzles. With a long-handled fork, place each cutlet into oil. Be careful: Oil will pop. Fry 3 to 5 minutes on each side, depending on size of cutlets. Remove from oil and drain on paper towels. To make gravy: Pour off all but 3 tbsp. oil from skillet, keeping browned bits in pan. Heat oil over medium heat. Sprinkle 1/2 cup flour over oil (use the flour mixture left over from dredging the cutlets, adding more flour as needed). Stir quickly with a wooden spoon to brown flour.

Combine milk and water and gradually add to skillet, stirring constantly and mashing any lumps. Lower heat and continue stirring until gravy reaches desired thickness. Taste and add more salt and pepper if necessary.

Serves 4

Lobster and Wild Mushroom Pasta

2	tbsp. minced garlic
1/2 cup	sliced onion
1 cup	Sherry Cream Sauce
1/2 cup	sliced shiitake mushrooms
1-1/2 cups	sliced Portobello mushrooms
1 cup	sliced white mushrooms
10 oz.	diced cooked lobster meat
1/2 cup	sugar snap peas
14 oz.	cooked penne pasta (1/2 of a 1-lb. box)
1-2 tbsp.	olive oil
	salt and pepper, to taste

Sherry Cream Sauce

1/2 cup	sherry
1 pint	heavy cream
1/4 cup	minced garlic
1/2 tbsp.	olive oil
1 tsp.	cornstarch, if desired
	water, as needed
	salt and pepper, to taste

To make sauce: Sauté garlic in olive oil. Deglaze pan with sherry. Add heavy cream, and simmer. Season with salt and pepper. If it is not thick enough for your taste, mix cornstarch with water to a slurry and add, making sure to continue simmering the sauce till the cornstarch thickens it. Set aside. (This recipe will make more sauce than you'll need, but it's good to have on hand. Store any extra in the refrigerator.) Sauté garlic and onion in olive oil. Add mushrooms and cook several minutes. Add Sherry Cream Sauce, lobster meat and snap peas and cook until heated through. Toss with pasta. Season with salt and pepper.

Serves 2

Miso-Crusted Salmon

2	6-oz salmon fillets
1/2 cup	Miso Marinade
1/4 cup	minced ginger
1/4 cup	minced garlic
1/2 cup	snap peas
1/2 cup	bean sprouts
1/2 cup	julienned red bell pepper
1/4 cup	olive oil
1 cup	baby bok choy
	salt and pepper, to taste

Miso Marinade

1-1/2 cups	miso
1-1/4 cups	sugar
1-1/4 cup	mirin
1 tbsp.	lemon juice
1 cup	cooking sake

Preheat oven to 350 degrees. To make the marinade: Combine marinade ingredients. (This recipe will make more marinade than you'll need, but it's good to have on hand. Store any extra in the refrigerator.) Sauté salmon fillets. Mix miso marinade with minced ginger; spread fillets with mixture and place in a baking pan. Bake until a crust forms, about 25 minutes. Sauté garlic, snap peas, bean sprouts, red pepper and bok choy in olive oil. Season with salt and pepper. Serve salmon on top of vegetables.

Serves 2

Lobster Newburg

4	cooked, shucked lobsters (1 to 2 lbs. each)
1/4 cup	clarified butter
1	shallot, finely minced
1 tsp.	white wine Worcestershire sauce
1 tsp.	black pepper
1/2 cup	sherry
2 tbsp.	paprika

White Sauce

4 cups	milk
2 sticks	butter or margarine
1 cup	flour
1 tbsp.	Dijon mustard
1/2 cup	lobster stock

To make white sauce: In the top of a 2-quart double boiler, heat milk to just before boiling. Meanwhile, melt butter or margarine in small saucepan. Add flour and mix thoroughly with a wire whisk. Slowly add this roux to the scalded milk, stirring constantly with whisk. Keep whisking to prevent lumps as sauce thickens. Add Dijon mustard and then lobster stock, slowly whisking after each addition until smooth. Set aside. Cut lobster into bite-sized pieces. Place clarified butter and minced shallot in a large sauté pan and cook on low heat until shallot is slightly browned. Add lobster pieces. Cook about 1 minute; add Worcestershire sauce and pepper. While stirring constantly with a wooden spoon, add sherry and cook until mixture starts to boil, about 2 minutes. Sprinkle with paprika and stir in white sauce. Reduce heat and simmer 2 minutes. Remove from heat.

Serves 8

PIGS' EARS AND OTHER DELICACIES

At the first tailgate show I hosted, I really didn't know what to expect. I knew I had to find interesting tailgates and interview the "chefs." On an incredibly hot and humid Saturday afternoon, Aloha Stadium was bursting at the seams with cars, and tailgaters were grilling almost on top of one another. We were supposed to be traveling through the parking lot in a golf cart, but the area was just gridlocked, so I left the cart (and the radio equipment) behind and took off with a cell phone. Walking through crowds of enthusiastic fans, breathing in kiawe wood smoke and stopping to interview some of the more exotic tailgaters, it occurred to me that I was about to discover more about local food in this parking lot than I would learn in 10 years of eating out in restaurants.

I wasn't wrong. That first day I tried pigs' ears (still with the little hairy bits on their tips) and bulls' testicles, better known to those who love them as rocky mountain oysters. People were anxious to give me everything they were eating, and I tried it all. To this day, I've never refused anything that's been offered to me when tailgating. No matter how unpalatable it might sound. Remember, I'm from the country that invented haggis!

Fred DeAngelo

Fred DeAngelo is one of the most pleasant and enthusiastic chefs I have ever worked with. He is also committed to supporting local farmers, and as the chef/partner of Tiki's Grill and Bar in Waikīkī, he produces a menu that features an abundance of local fish and produce—at extremely reasonable prices. Finally, like all of the chefs featured here, he loves to get outside and use the grill. Whenever Fred tailgates with us, we know we're in for a treat. He always brings along a small army of family and friends to help out, and his food is outstandingly good. It draws rave reviews from everyone who tries it, and I know you'll agree that the recipes he shared with us for this book are fabulous.

He grew up in a family where cooking was important and says he was in the kitchen by the age of six. Like many of our chefs, he first became interested in cooking when a loving grandmother instilled in him a love for great food and wine. Those food memories are some of the things that he carries with him today, and they really come through in his work. Something else I love about Fred is that he really gets how lucky we are to live and work in Hawai'i. Find him early in the morning looking over the lanai from Tiki's to the stunning blue of Waikīkī's waters, and you just know he's already having a good day. Whether he's in his restaurant or out in the parking lot, he's always a pleasure to work with.

The dessert recipes from Tiki's are provided by Ron Villoria, the restaurant's talented pastry chef.

5-Spice-Braised Beef Short Ribs

12	beef short ribs (3-bone, each 3 to 4 inches thick)
	5-Spice Seasoned Salt
6 tbsp.	vegetable oil
3	onions, cut in 1-by-1-inch pieces
3	carrots, peeled and chopped in 1-inch pieces
1 bunch	celery, chopped
12	garlic cloves
5	bay leaves
2 tbsp.	dried rosemary
2 cups	red wine
2 qts.	veal or beef stock
1 cup	butter
1 cup	flour
1/4 cup	hoisin sauce
	salt and pepper, to taste

5-Spice Seasoned Salt

2 oz. (1/2 cup plus 1 tbsp.)	Chinese 5-spice
2 oz. (3/4 cup)	salt
2 oz. (scant cup)	black pepper

Preheat oven to 350 degrees. Using a boning knife, remove 2 of the 3 bones on the short ribs. Use kitchen twine to tie in a circular shape surrounding the remaining bone. To make seasoned salt: Combine ingredients. Any leftover seasoned salt can be saved. Season with 5-spice-seasoned salt. Heat oil over medium heat and sear all sides of the short ribs in an oven-proof braising pan. Remove from pan. Add onion, carrot and celery to same braising pan. Cook until onion is translucent. Add garlic and dried herbs. Deglaze pan with wine, and simmer until liquid is reduced by 1/3. Add stock and bring to a boil. Add short ribs, making sure the liquid covers the meat. Cover pan tightly with foil, and place lid on pan. Braise about 1-1/2 hours, until meat is fork-tender. Uncover pan, remove foil and allow ribs to rest 15 minutes. Remove ribs from liquid. Place liquid into blender; pulse 3 times and strain. To make sauce: Melt butter in a saucepan over medium heat, then add flour and stir well to make a roux; do not burn. Add strained braising liquid, bring to a slow simmer and allow to thicken. Add hoisin sauce, taste and adjust seasonings.

Serves 12

| NOTE | *These ribs may be cooked a day ahead. At the tailgate you can reheat them over low heat on a grill or in a pot on the grill, with some stock. Serve with sauce, seasonal vegetables and mashed potatoes. Try infusing the mashed potato with roasted garlic, a corn relish, or even pesto for a change of flavor.*

Island Cioppino

1/4 cup	olive oil
8	scallops
4	4-oz. pieces moi, mahimahi or snapper
8	mussels
12	clams
1 cup	white wine
12	shrimp, peeled and deveined

Cioppino Sauce

5 tbsp.	olive oil
3/4 cup	julienned Maui onion
3/4 cup	julienned red bell pepper
1/4 cup	celery, chopped
1 tbsp.	minced garlic
1/2 tsp.	dried oregano
1/2 tsp.	crushed red pepper
1-1/2 cups	fish stock or clam juice
1-1/2 lbs.	canned tomatoes (whole, peeled, in juice), crushed by hand, juice reserved
1 tsp.	chopped Italian parsley
1/2 cup	white wine
	salt and pepper, to taste

Make sauce the night before. Heat olive oil in a large pot over medium heat. Add onion, bell pepper and celery; sauté 3 minutes. Add garlic, oregano, red pepper, salt and pepper; sauté 2 minutes, being careful not to burn garlic. Add fish stock, tomato and parsley; simmer 10 minutes. Cool and refrigerate. At the tailgate: Over high heat, heat olive oil and sear scallops 1 minute; add fish, sauté another minute; add mussels and clams. Deglaze pan with wine; add cioppino sauce and shrimp. Simmer 3 to 5 minutes, until clams and mussels open and fish is just cooked through.

Serves 4

Tiki's Crab Cakes

2 lbs.	Dungeness crabmeat
1/2 cup	diced red bell pepper
1/2 cup	diced green bell peppers
1/2 cup	yellow bell peppers
1/4 cup	pasteurized egg yolk (or 1 fresh egg yolk)
1 squeeze	lime juice
2 tsp.	sweet Thai chili sauce
	salt and pepper, to taste
1 cup	seasoned flour (1 cup flour, 2 tsp. salt, 2 tsp. white pepper)
1 cup	egg wash (egg beaten in water)
1 cup	panko (Japanese breadcrumbs)
6 tbsp.	drawn butter

Shell-Stock Cream Reduction

1 cup	heavy cream
1/2 cup	shrimp stock (can substitute shrimp base)

To make shell-stock cream: Simmer cream and stock until reduced to 1/2 cup. Refrigerate. Drain liquid from crabmeat. Add peppers, egg yolk, shell stock cream, lime juice, chili sauce, salt and pepper. Mix well and chill 1 hour. Form into 2 oz wt. balls. Dust with seasoned flour, dip in egg wash, and then cover completely with panko. Sauté over medium heat in drawn butter to reach an internal temperature of 130 degrees. Serve with tarter sauce, lemon butter, or sweet chili sauce.

Serves 12

Shrimp Penne

6 tbsp.	olive oil
1 lb.	Crimini or button mushrooms, sliced
1/2 cup	minced garlic
2 lbs.	shrimp (21- to 25-count size), cleaned and deveined
1 tsp.	crushed red pepper flakes, or more to taste
1 tbsp.	lemon zest
1 lb.	Haula Tomato Concase, diced (about 6 tomatoes)
1/2 cup plus 2 tbsp.	white wine
1/2 cup plus 2 tbsp.	shrimp stock or clam juice
6 lbs.	penne pasta, cooked al dente (3 lbs. dry)
1 stick	butter, at room temperature, or more to taste
1/4 cup	sweet basil, chopped
1/4 cup	chopped Italian parsley
1 squeeze	lemon juice
	salt and pepper, to taste

To prepare concase: Cut an X into the tops of tomatoes. Remove cores. Bring a pot of water to boil and prepare an ice bath. Place no more than 3 tomatoes at a time in the boiling water. Boil 4 seconds, then immediately shock in ice water. Remove skin, cut in half and remove seeds and pulp. This may be done the night before. Dice before using. At the tailgate: Heat oil in a large wok over medium-high heat. Add mushrooms and cook 45 seconds. Add garlic (do not burn), shrimp, crushed pepper, lemon zest and tomato concase. Deglaze wok with wine and stock. Reduce until liquid forms a light glaze. Add pasta; season with salt and pepper. Add butter and toss. Stir in basil; top with parsley and a squeeze of lemon.

Serves 12 or more

NOTE *To save time on tailgating day, cook the pasta a day ahead. Toss with olive oil and salt and refrigerate overnight.*

Chocolate Coconut Bread Pudding

1 loaf	brioche, cubed (or 6 large croissants, torn apart)

Caramel Base

2 cups	sugar

Custard

8 oz.	dark chocolate, chopped
2 cups	milk
2 cups	coconut milk
1	vanilla bean
3/4 cup	sugar
8	eggs
1 cup	shredded coconut

To make caramel base: Cook sugar in a sauté pan, stirring constantly, until it melts and turns amber, making a caramel. Carefully pour into a 9-by-9-inch baking pan or ceramic dish. Tilt pan so caramel coats the bottom. Cool. Preheat oven to 350 degrees. Add cubed bread to pan. To make custard: Bring milk, coconut milk and vanilla bean to a boil. Whisk sugar and eggs together in a separate dish. Pour hot milk into egg mixture while whisking. While the custard mixture is still hot, add the chopped chocolate and stir until it is melted. Pour custard mixture over bread cubes and allow bread to soak it up. Sprinkle with coconut. Bake 50 minutes to 1 hour. Cool 1 hour before serving. May be served warm or chilled.

Serves 8-9

Banana Upside-Down Cake

5-6	bananas
1 stick	butter
1-3/4 cups	powdered sugar
1 tbsp.	vanilla
5	eggs
1-3/4 cups	flour, sifted
2-1/2 tsp.	baking powder, sifted

Topping

1 stick	butter
2 cups	brown sugar
1/4 cup	rum

Preheat oven to 350 degrees. Grease an 8-inch cake pan. To make topping: Heat butter and sugar in a pan, stirring occasionally. When sugar comes to a boil, add rum. Remove from heat and pour into the cake pan, covering bottom of pan evenly. Slice bananas in half lengthwise. Place in pan, cut side down, until bottom of pan is covered. Cream together butter, sugar and vanilla. Add eggs one at a time. Fold in flour and baking powder. Pour over bananas in pan, spreading evenly. Bake 45 to 50 minutes, until a toothpick inserted in the center of the cake comes out clean. Run a paring knife or small spatula around edge of cake to loosen. Cool 15 minutes. While cake is still warm, invert a serving plate on top of cake pan and turn cake upside-down onto plate. Unmold. Cool 30 minutes, then refrigerate. May be served chilled or at room temperature.

Serves 8

Apple Crumb Pie

1	9-inch pie shell

Filling

3 pounds	Granny Smith apples, peeled, cored and cubed
1/4 cup	sugar
1 tsp.	cinnamon
1/4 tsp.	nutmeg
3 tbsp.	flour
1 tbsp.	butter, cut in small pieces
1 pinch	salt
	juice of 1 lemon

Crumble

8 tbsp.	butter
1-1/4 cups	sugar
	zest of 1 lemon
2-1/4 cups	flour
1/4 cup	Parmesan cheese

Preheat oven to 350 degrees. Combine filling ingredients in a large bowl. Place crumble ingredients in a separate bowl and mix by hand until mixture resembles a coarse meal. Place filling in pie shell. Top with an even layer of crumble mixture. Bake 45 to 50 minutes. Cool on a rack for 1 hour. May be served chilled or warm.

Serves 8

Banana Cheesecake

1 lb.	cream cheese
3/4 cup	sugar
4	eggs
1 cup	sour cream
1 cup	puréed bananas
1 cup	sour cream, for topping
	juice of 1 lemon

Crust

2 cups	graham cracker crumbs
1/4 cup	butter, melted

Caramelized Bananas

5	bananas
1/2 cup	sugar

Grease an 8-inch cake pan. Combine crust ingredients and line bottom of pan. Refrigerate. Preheat oven to 325 degrees. Cream the cream cheese and sugar until smooth. Add lemon juice and eggs, one at a time. Mix in sour cream and bananas. Pour batter over crust and place in a large roasting pan. Fill roasting pan with water until it reaches 1/4 of the cake pan height. Bake 1 to 1-1/4 hours. To caramelize bananas: Slice bananas in half lengthwise and sprinkle cut sides with sugar. Heat a sauté pan on medium high heat with a small amount of butter. Place bananas in pan, sugared side down, and cook until they caramelize. Remove from heat and reserve. Remove cheesecake from oven and top with remaining sour cream while cake is still hot. Cool 1 hour, then refrigerate. Unmold and top with caramelized bananas.

Serves 8

THE STADIUM SCENE

There are people who tailgate at Aloha Stadium who have been there for as long as the parking lot has existed. There are others who come for just a game or two a year, and there are those who meet up with old friends only to share a meal and a beer in the lot and then lose touch again until the next year.

There's a camaraderie amongst tailgaters. A feeling of "family" when really, these are people you park your car next to for a football season that sometimes has only eight home games. But for dedicated tailgaters, those afternoons in the parking lot represent something special. Time to talk. Time to catch up on family and friends. Time to watch the kids grow—as they seem to, before your very eyes. That happens when you see them just one season a year.

These bonded tailgaters take their food seriously, too, and it's common to find groups who have a weekly theme to their parties. When Rice comes to town, you'll find every rice dish on the planet, and the phrase "we're going to eat Rice" is heard a hundred times over.

When Alabama came to town a few years ago they brought 10,000 fans with them—all of them, it seemed to me, experts on Southern food. But no matter how far they come, how much food they bring and how experienced they think they are, everyone agrees—they've never seen food at a tailgate quite like Hawai'i's.

Elmer Guzman

If you want to know about local fish, you have to go find Elmer Guzman. He grew up on Maui and has never lost his love of the kind of dishes his mom used to make with reef fish. He's worked under Alan Wong, Emeril Lagasse and Sam Choy, and he'll be the first person to tell you that he's learned a lot from all three.

But Elmer has his own style. I wrote, years ago when I first tasted his food, that he was going to be one of the next generation of famous chefs in Hawai'i, and I believe that is already coming true. He has a fantastic way with food, and I'm sure he's destined for great things.

When Elmer joins us for a tailgate there are several things you'll see. One is his wife Samantha, who is constantly by his side, supporting him in everything. The second is that Elmer is as excited about being at a UH football game as we are about having him cook. He's a true UH fan, and he doesn't miss a thing when it comes to talking sports. The third thing you're guaranteed to see at Elmer's tailgate is fish. Lots of it. And lots of fun, too.

It's impossible to say who our most popular tailgate chef is—all of them are so fabulous—but Elmer is definitely one who creates a lot of excitement in the parking lot. And if you enjoy the recipes he shared with us here, you'll love his own cookbook, *The Shoreline Chef: Creative Cuisine for Hawaiian Reef Fish*.

Charboiled Whole Kumu

5-6	whole kumu (12 oz. each)
	salt and fresh cracked pepper, to taste

All-Purpose Herb Oil

1 cup	extra virgin olive oil
2 sprigs	fresh thyme
2 sprigs	fresh rosemary
3 cloves	garlic, smashed
1 tsp.	whole black peppercorns
1	bay leaf

Garlic Butter for Seafood

1 lb.	softened unsalted butter
1/4 cup	white wine (optional)
1/4 cup	minced garlic
1 tsp.	minced parsley
	splash of Tabasco sauce
	splash of Worcestershire sauce
	juice of 1 lemon

To make herb oil: Combine all ingredients and let sit at least 24 hours. To make garlic butter: Combine ingredients well. Season fish with salt and fresh cracked pepper. Marinate in herb oil 1 hour. Grill fish over medium heat, basting periodically with garlic butter, 20-30 minutes.

Serves 4-6

| NOTE | *The garlic butter used to baste this grilled dish both seasons the fish and keeps it moist.*

Local-Style Foil-Wrapped Whole Uhu

4-5 lbs.	whole uhu
1 cup	mayonnaise
4 oz.	sliced Portuguese sausage
1	sliced lemon
1	sliced medium onion
1	ti leaf
1	sheet foil, large enough to wrap fish
1/4 cup	minced ginger
1 cup	chopped cilantro
1 cup	sliced green onion
6 tbsp.	shoyu
2 tbsp.	sesame oil
	salt and pepper, to taste

Preheat oven to 350 degrees. Score fish by making diagonal cuts 1 inch apart, all the way to the bone, creating 1-inch diamonds on both sides. Season inside and out with salt and pepper. Rub mayonnaise in the score marks and cavity. Tuck sausage, lemon and sliced onion in the score marks. Place ti leaf in the center of foil sheet. Place fish on ti leaf. Sprinkle remaining ingredients evenly over fish. Gather edges of foil to the center and crimp tight to prevent steam from escaping. Bake 45 minutes to 1 hour.

Serves 4-6

| NOTE | *This easy-to-prepare dish can go right from the oven to the table in its foil container.*

Grilled Butaguchi with Charred Jalapeno Corn Relish

4	butaguchi fillets (5 oz. each, from 5- to 6-lb. whole fish)
1/4 cup	All-Purpose Herb Oil (see page 30)
	Garlic Butter for Seafood (see page 30)
	salt and pepper, to taste

Charred Jalapeno Corn Relish

2 cups	charred corn kernels (grill 4 ears of shucked corn 5-10 minutes, turning periodically; cut kernels off cobs)
1/2 cup	diced red bell peppers
1/2 cup	diced red onions
1 cup	sliced green onions
2	minced jalapenos
1 cup	mayonnaise
	juice of 1/2 lemon
	minced cilantro (optional)

To make relish: Combine all ingredients and chill. Marinate fillets in herb oil for 10 to 15 minutes. Season with salt and pepper. Grill 3-4 minutes on each side. Top each fillet with a dollop of garlic butter. Serve with relish.

Serves 4-6

| NOTE | *Grilled corn adds a distinct smoky flavor to the relish that complements this dish.*

Filipino-Influenced Moi Ceviche

16 oz.	moi sashimi
1/4 tsp.	thinly sliced shallots (may substitute yellow onions)
1/4 oz.	
1 tbsp.	thinly sliced green onion
1/4 cup	minced ginger
2 tbsp.	calamansi juice
	Chinese soy sauce
	sweet chili sauce, to taste
	salt and black pepper, to taste

Layer moi sashimi on a plate. Arrange shallots, green onion and ginger over moi. Pour calamansi juice over moi, then soy sauce. Dot each piece of fish with sweet chili sauce; sprinkle with salt and pepper. Let sit for 10-15 minutes before serving.

Serves 4-6

| NOTE | *The citrus juice of the calamansi is normally used as a condiment with the Filipino noodle dish known as pancit bihai. In this dish, it is used to lightly season the moi, as are the Chinese soy sauce and Thai sweet chili sauce.*

Wayne Hirabayashi

Although Wayne Hirabayashi has daily access to a kiawe-wood grill, a tandoori oven and a wood-burning pizza oven, he still can't resist the call of the barbecue grill. At Hoku's, the award-winning signature restaurant at the Kahala Mandarin Oriental, he creates stunning dishes that are a blend of Asian and local flavors. He brings exactly the same style and flair to tailgating.

Wayne was born and raised in Hawai'i and is a graduate of the prestigious Culinary Institute of America in New York; though he's worked around the world, it's obvious to anyone who knows him that he's most comfortable with the flavors and the friend-ships of Hawai'i.

I think he's possibly the hardest-working chef I know, and one of the reasons we love having him tailgate with us every year is that we're able to "treat" him to a day away from his hectic schedule and to tickets to the game. He always jokes that without tailgating he'd never get out to Aloha Stadium.

In terms of presentation and style and just how many dishes he makes for a tailgate, Wayne is one of the most creative chefs ever to hit the barbecue. Certainly some of our most memorable tailgates have been with him—and as well as the food, everyone always enjoys his personality. We hope that we'll always have him tailgating with us. Try his Ahi Poke Dip recipe (on page 37), and you'll see why.

Champagne Vinaigrette-Grilled Pepper-Crusted Rare Tuna

6 blocks	ahi, 2-1/2 oz. each
1/2 cup	daikon threads (slice with Japanese vegetable slicer)
1/2 cup	prepared seaweed salad
1/2 cup	Chinese peas, blanched and julienned
6 tbsp.	Champagne Vinaigrette, or a prepared vinaigrette
1/2 cup	Soy Ginger Vinaigrette
	julienned red chili pepper, for garnish
	sliced green onion, for garnish
	Hawaiian salt, to taste
	coarsely ground white pepper, to taste
	lemon juice, to taste
	vegetable oil

Champagne Vinaigrette

1/2 cup	Champagne vinegar
1 tbsp.	minced garlic
1 tbsp.	honey
2 tbsp.	minced shallots
3/4 cup	vegetable oil
6 tbsp.	chicken stock
6 tbsp.	water
3 tbsp.	sugar
	salt and fresh-ground white pepper, to taste

Soy-Ginger Vinaigrette

1 cup	shoyu
1/2 cup plus 2 tbsp.	rice wine vinegar
1/4 cup	mirin
2 tbsp.	lime juice
1/4 cup	sugar
1 tsp.	minced ginger
1 tsp.	chopped garlic
1/2 tsp.	sesame oil
1/4 tsp.	ground white pepper
1/2 tsp.	chili paste (sambal), or to taste

To make Champagne vinaigrette: Place vinegar, garlic, honey, pepper and shallots in deep container. Mix with hand blender until well blended. Strain. Slowly add oil and mix until emulsified. Add chicken stock, water, salt and white pepper; blend again. Adjust seasonings. Refrigerate until needed. Makes about 2 cups (more than needed, but it's good to have around). To make Soy-Ginger Vinaigrette: Place all ingredients in a stainless-steel container; mix well and let sit at room temperature for 2 hours. You can strain it after this if you don't want it too hot. Adjust seasonings and refrigerate (it will keep up to 3 to 4 days). Makes a little over 2 cups—again, you won't need so much for this recipe, but it's good to have around! Prepare a grill. Season fish well with Hawaiian salt, white pepper and lemon juice; brush with oil. Grill until rare. Combine vegetables in bowl and toss lightly with Champagne vinaigrette. Season them with salt and pepper and place them in the center of a plate. Top with ahi and spoon soy ginger vinaigrette on top. Garnish with chili and green onion. Serve immediately.

Serves 2 as an entrée or 6 as an appetizer

Warm Salad of Kiawe-Grilled Pacific Salmon, with Sweet Kahuku Watermelon Salsa

20-oz.	Pacific salmon fillet, skin on, cut in 4 strips
1/4 cup	olive oil
4 cups	Waimanalo greens
1/4 cup	roasted pumpkin seed oil
1/4 cup	herb oil
	juice of 2 lemons
	alaʻe (Hawaiian red sea salt), to taste
	freshly ground white pepper, to taste

Watermelon Salsa

1 cup	diced, seedless Kahuku watermelon
2 tbsp.	minced Maui onion
1 tsp.	roughly chopped cilantro
1 tbsp.	finely sliced green onion
1 tbsp.	jalapeno pepper, minced
1 tsp.	green Tabasco
	juice of 2 limes

To make salsa: Combine ingredients and mix well; refrigerate. Prepare a grill. Season salmon with salt and pepper. Brush with olive oil. Grill skin-side down until crisp. Turn and grill another 2 minutes, or until done. Keep warm. Toss greens with pumpkin seed oil and lemon juice and season lightly with salt and pepper. Place salad in a mound on a plate. Place the salmon next to it. Place salsa next to salmon, and drizzle it with herb oil. Serve with your favorite chips.

Serves 4

Ahi Poke Dip

8 oz.	sushi-grade ahi, diced
4 cups	mayonnaise
1/2 cup	shoyu
1/4 tsp.	minced garlic
1/2 cup	minced pickled ginger
2 tbsp.	roughly chopped cilantro
1 cup	minced scallions
1 cup	lightly whipped cream

Combine everything except whipped cream and mix well. Fold in whipped cream. Mixture will keep, refrigerated, for up to 2 days.

Makes 2 qts.

Ahi Poke Musubi with King Crab Namasu

Sushi Rice

1/2 cup	rice vinegar
6 tbsp.	sugar
3 tsp.	salt
1 cup	rice

Ahi Poke

1/4 cup	diced ahi
1 tbsp.	minced green onion
1 tbsp.	finely sliced Maui onion
1 tbsp.	roughly chopped ogo
	sesame oil, to taste
	ala'e (Hawaiian red sea salt), to taste
	chili water, to taste
	'inamona (ground kukui nut), to taste

Crab Namasu

1/4 cup	Japanese cucumber, seeds removed, in 1/4-inch slices, lightly salted for 1 hour and drained
2 tbsp.	daikon, in 1/4-inch slices
1 tbsp.	sliced green onion
2 tbsp.	king crab meat, picked clean of shells and squeezed of excess liquid (keep chunky)
1/4 cup	Namasu Marinade
	salt, to taste

Namasu marinade

1-3/4 cups	rice vinegar
3/4 cup	sugar, or to taste
1 tbsp.	finely chopped ginger
	salt, to taste

To complete dish

1/4 cup · furikake
2 cups · vegetable oil, for frying
2 tbsp. · ponzu mayonnaise (see note)
baby romaine leaves (enough to cover as
many plates as you're using)

To make sushi rice: Cook rice. Combine vinegar, sugar and salt in a saucepan. Warm over low heat to dissolve sugar. Remove from heat and cool; toss with rice. To make poke: Combine all ingredients and mix well. Taste and adjust seasonings. To make namasu: Combine marinade ingredients. Toss with remaining ingredients; mix well. To make musubi: Spread sushi rice 2 inches thick inside musubi molds. Place 2 tbsp. poke in center of each layer of rice. Cover poke with remaining rice. Heat oil to 350 degrees. Coat each musubi with furikake. Deep-fry. Cut in halves or quarters. Arrange romaine leaves in a circle on individual plates. Place namasu in center. Drizzle with ponzu mayonnaise. Tuck pieces of musubi between romaine leaves.

Serves 2 to 4, as an appetizer

| NOTE | *Ponzu mayonnaise can be bought at Asian food stores.*

D.K. Kodama

I first met D.K. Kodama years ago. He was the chef-owner of a terrific restaurant on Maui and about to get married to his sweetheart Lori. Since then, he's opened three additional restaurants: Sansei Seafood Restaurant and Sushi Bar at Restaurant Row on Oahu; Vino, serving rustic Italian food and great wine on Maui; and little Vino on Oʻahu. He and Lori now have two children, and the family theme continues to dominate his work. He's devoted, of course, to Lori and his kids, but a sense of family permeates almost everything D.K. and his team do. His mom and dad are at the Honolulu restaurant every day, and everyone who works for the Kodamas or even visits them as a guest gets a sense of a really close-knit family.

D.K. and the team from Sansei are always popular guests at our tailgates, and they really show how simple it is to make good food on the grill. "If you use a grill correctly, the food can be awesome," says D.K. He proves that every time he tailgates with us—and every day at his expanding chain of restaurants. Tom Selman, a key member of his team, is responsible for many of the recipes here, and I love how he manages to bring a sense of comfort food to some new-wave dishes. Try the chicken dish here with Tom's mashed potatoes, and you'll see exactly what I mean.

By the time you read this book, there should be two more of D.K.'s restaurants open in Hawaiʻi—a steak house in Waikīkī and another seafood restaurant and sushi bar. We just hope that D.K. and his team don't get too busy to spend some time each summer cooking out with us.

Crystallized Baby Back Ribs

2	racks baby back ribs

Marinade

1/2 cup	chili powder
1 tbsp.	minced garlic
1/2 tsp.	chopped fresh thyme
1 piece	star anise
1 slice	ginger, peeled (1/2-inch by 2-inch)
2 cups	shoyu
1 cup	balsamic vinaigrette
1 cup	olive oil
1 cup	vegetable oil

Honey Mustard Sauce

1/4 cup	Dijon mustard
1 tbsp.	red wine vinegar
1/2 cup	packed brown sugar

To prepare marinade: Combine chili powder, garlic, thyme, star anise, ginger, shoyu and vinegar in a bowl. Slowly whisk in olive oil and vegetable oil until mixture is thickened. Marinade may be stored in an airtight container, refrigerated, for up to 1 month. Place ribs in a shallow dish and pour marinade over them. Turn to coat well. Cover and refrigerate overnight. Preheat oven to 400 degrees. Transfer ribs to roasting pan. Bake, covered, 60 to 90 minutes, until meat starts to fall off the bone. Remove ribs from oven and brush with honey mustard sauce. Sprinkle sugar over ribs. Carefully wave a lit butane torch over ribs to caramelize sugar, or place ribs under a hot broiler just long enough to caramelize sugar, about 5 minutes. Watch closely, as sugar burns easily.

Serves 4

Miso Butterfish

4	boneless butterfish fillets, 6 oz. each, skin on
1/2 cup	Su-Miso Sauce
1 cup	chopped fresh chives, for garnish
1 tbsp.	shichimi (seven-spice powder), for garnish

Su-Miso Sauce

1/4 cup	mirin (sweet rice wine)
1/2 cup	sake
2 cups	sugar
1-1/4 cups	white miso

Miso Marinade

1/2 cup	white miso
1/2 cup	sugar
2 tbsp.	mirin
2 tbsp.	sake

To make Su-Miso Sauce: In a saucepan, cook mirin and sake over high heat until alcohol cooks off, about 4 minutes. Decrease heat to medium, add sugar and stir until dissolved. Whisk in miso. Remove from heat and let cool. Store in an airtight container, refrigerated, up to 1 month. Leftover sauce may be served with other fish or chicken dishes. To make marinade: Combine miso and sugar in a bowl and mix well. Add mirin and sake, mixing until smooth. May be stored in an airtight container, refrigerated, up to 1 month. Place butterfish in shallow dish and cover with marinade. Turn to coat well; cover and refrigerate at least 12 hours. Preheat oven to 400 degrees. Remove fillets from marinade, shaking off excess liquid, and transfer to baking pan. Bake until skin is crisp, about 10 minutes. To serve, spoon 2 tbsp. Su-Miso Sauce on each of 4 plates and place 1 fillet on top of each. Sprinkle with chives and shichimi.

Serves 4

Japanese-Style Jerk Chicken

2	whole fryers, split in half
2 tbsp.	shichimi (seven-spice powder)
3 tbsp.	chopped fresh chives, for garnish

Marinade

2	chili peppers, crushed
1 cup	shoyu
1	lemon, halved
4 cups	water
	juice of 1 lemon

Sauce

1/4 cup	sake
3 cups	assorted vegetables (celery, carrots, onions, etc.), cut into 1-inch chunks
1-1/2 cups	chicken broth
1-1/2 tbsp.	unsalted butter, at room temperature
	kosher salt and fresh-ground black pepper, to taste
	juice of 1 lemon

Place the chicken in a shallow dish. Combine marinade ingredients and pour over chicken. Cover and marinate in refrigerator overnight. Prepare fire in charcoal grill or preheat gas grill. Preheat oven to 400 degrees. Season chicken with the shichimi. Place on grill rack and sear, skin side down, 4 to 5 minutes, until nicely marked. Transfer to ungreased roasting pan and bake 15 minutes, until skin is brown and crisp and juices run clear. Remove from pan and set aside. To make sauce: Set roasting pan over medium-high heat. Add sake and lemon juice, stirring to loosen browned bits from sides and bottom of pan. Add vegetables. Decrease heat to medium and cook until jus tender, about 6 minutes. Add broth and simmer until liquid is reduced by a quarter, about 4 minutes. Stir in butter and season with salt and pepper. To serve: This is good with Garlic Mashed Potatoes (recipe follows). Divide mashed potatoes among 4 large serving bowls. Divide chicken pieces by pulling breast away from leg. In each bowl place a scoop of mashed potatoes, topped with a quarter of chicken. Place vegetables on top of chicken. Ladle sauce over all and top with chives.

Serves 4

Garlic Mashed Potatoes

1-1/2 lbs.	Yukon Gold potatoes, peeled and diced into 1-inch cubes
3 cloves	roasted garlic (see note)
1 cup	heavy cream
2 tbsp.	unsalted butter, at room temperature
	kosher salt and freshly ground pepper, to taste

In a large saucepot, bring 1/2 gallon of salted water to a boil. Add potatoes and cook 20 minutes, until fork-tender. Drain. In a small saucepan, bring cream just to a boil. Remove from heat and set aside. Mash potatoes with garlic, cream and butter until creamy. Season with salt and pepper.

Serves 4

| NOTE | *Roasted garlic is available in supermarkets, or you can make it yourself by brushing a head of garlic with olive oil and baking, covered, for 20 minutes in a 400-degree oven. The garlic will turn soft and sweet.*

Chef Tom Selman's Macadamia Nut-Smoked Beef Brisket

1	whole beef brisket (5 to 8 pounds)
4 cups	macadamia nut shells

Marinade

1 cup	shoyu
2 cups	olive oil
1 tbsp.	chopped garlic
1 tbsp.	sliced ginger
1/2 cup	sugar
1 cup	red wine

Combine marinade ingredients. Place brisket in a pan big enough to hold it and the marinade. Pour marinade over brisket, cover and refrigerate overnight or at least 6 hours. Start fire and place macadamia nut shells in a smoker box. When shells are smoking, place brisket over smoker and smoke 4 to 6 hours. (Temperature should stay at about 300 degrees. Monitor temperature so grill doesn't get too hot.) Serve with bread, rice, macaroni salad, and coleslaw.

Serves 16

| NOTE | *To save time, brisket may be cut into 2-inch-thick strips before marinating. Marinate 2 hours; smoke 2 hours. The most important part of this dish is the slow smoking of the meat. Temperature regulation is key. You want long, low and slow cooking. About 300 degrees for 4 hours should result in a smoky, juicy product.*

George Mavrothalassitis

George Mavrothalassitis gives new meaning to the word "passion." Whether he's talking about local fish, the latest food-and-wine pairing at his restaurant, or his Harley-Davidson motorcycle, there's an almost tangible air of excitement around him.

He was born in the port of Marseilles and has never forgotten the flavors and influences of his homeland. He's a James Beard Award winner, having picked up the prestigious Best Chef in Hawaii and Pacific Northwest in 2003, and he's a staunch supporter of local produce.

He has also spent a lot of time getting rid of, as he puts it, "the BS in my cooking." When I saw him recently, he told me excitedly about his latest grilling project, cooking simple roasted pig and barbecue for hundreds. His restaurant, Chef Mavro, on South King Street in Honolulu, has a unique food-and-wine-pairing menu that changes every few months, but he still takes time out from creating that to get out the grill or rise early enough to go to the fish auction to make sure that he stays in touch with everything that goes on in the local food world.

His recipes might seem a little daunting at first, but they're perfect for the tailgate where you want to surprise your guests and take the party to a whole new level.

Salad of Grilled Kahuku Prawns Marinated in Cumin, with Bulgur Tabbouleh and Bouquet of Watercress

2 lbs.	Kahuku prawns, 15-count size, head on, 3 to 4 per person
	watercress leaves, for garnish

Cumin Marinade

1/4 cup	ground, toasted coriander seed
1/4 cup	ground, toasted cumin
1/2 cup	shoyu
1-1/2 cups	extra virgin olive oil
6 cloves	garlic, crushed
1 tbsp.	Hawaiian salt
	pepper, to taste

Tabbouleh

1-1/2 cups	bulgur wheat
1 cup	tomato juice
1 cup	water
3	tomatoes, finely diced
1	purple onion, finely diced
3 tbsp.	finely minced mint leaves
3 tbsp.	chopped cilantro
1/4 cup	extra virgin olive oil
1	red bell pepper, diced
3 cups	finely diced pineapple
	juice of 2 limes
	salt and pepper, to taste

Combine marinade ingredients. Pour over prawns and marinate 2-3 hours. To make tabbouleh: Combine tomato juice and water, season with salt and pepper, and bring to a boil. Remove from heat. Add bulgur, mix well, cover and let sit for 30-45 minutes. Fluff with a fork and combine with other ingredients. Grill or bake prawns until pink. To serve: Arrange tabbouleh in a ring on each plate. Place watercress in center of ring. Surround tabbouleh with prawns.

Serves 8

Rotisserie Island Chicken and Kahuku Creamed Corn, Huli-Huli Style

1	Island roasting chicken
1/2 cup	prepared huli-huli sauce
1 tbsp.	Hawaiian salt
	pepper, to taste

Creamed Corn

1/2 cup	milk
1 tsp.	chopped garlic
1 tbsp.	butter
2 ears	Kahuku corn, kernels cut off

Sauce

1 tsp.	minced shallot
1 tsp.	chopped ginger
1 tsp.	chopped garlic
1 tsp.	cracked black pepper
1 cup	plum wine
1/2 cup	demi glace
1/2 cup	prepared huli-huli sauce
12	Hawaiian chilies
1 tsp.	sesame oil

Preheat oven to 375 degrees. Brush chicken with huli-huli sauce and season with Hawaiian salt and pepper. Roast chicken in a covered grill (stand chicken on an empty beer can). Brush occasionally with huli-huli sauce. To prepare corn: Sauté garlic in butter. Add corn and sauté until translucent. Cover with milk, then simmer for 5 minutes. Remove half the corn to a blender and blend until smooth. Return to pot with remaining corn; stir in butter. Season to taste.

To make sauce: Sauté shallot, ginger, garlic and black pepper. Add plum wine and simmer until liquid is evaporated. Add demiglace, huli-huli sauce and chilies. Stir sesame oil and strain. To serve: Remove breasts and legs of chicken from bone. Spoon corn onto 2 plates. Place a breast and leg on top of corn and surround with sauce.

Serves 2

Hawaiian Vanilla Bean Cheesecake

8 oz.	cream cheese
1/4 cup	Vanilla Bean Sugar
2	large eggs
5 tbsp.	vanilla extract

Crust

1-1/4 cups	graham cracker crumbs
2 tbsp.	sugar
1 tsp.	cinnamon
2 oz.	melted unsalted butter

Preheat oven to 300 degrees. To make vanilla bean sugar: Split a vanilla bean and bury it in a cup of sugar. Let sit for at least a week before using. More sugar can be added as the scented sugar is used. To make crust: Combine ingredients and press into bottom and sides of pie tin. Set aside. Beat eggs. In another bowl, cream the cream cheese with vanilla sugar and vanilla extract. Add eggs, mixing well. Pour filling into crust. Bake 25 minutes.

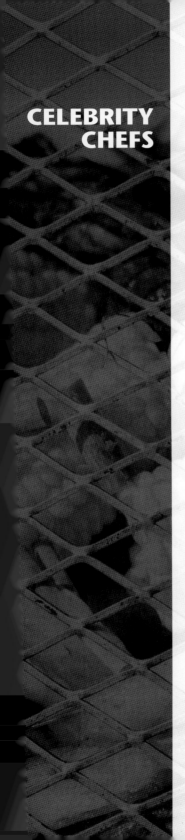

CELEBRITY CHEFS

About four years ago I decided that I wanted to see just how far tailgating could go. Jim Webb, then president of Gaspro, was keen to raise the bar at his increasingly large gatherings, and I thought of asking some chefs to participate. I was a little hesitant about calling the likes of Alan Wong, Philippe Padovani and Wayne Hirabayashi to see if they would mind driving out to the parking lot and cooking, but without exception, they all jumped at the chance. It turns out there's nothing that chefs like more than the opportunity to cook outside on an open grill. That first year we had nine chefs join us, and now we have a waiting list of people wanting to participate!

The chefs are outstanding, and it's great to see them away from their kitchen environments. One of the things I particularly enjoy is when the tailgate is over and we hand them tickets to the game. Chefs like Wayne Hirabayashi and Alan Wong rarely get time to take a Saturday off and watch UH play, and it's really a thrill to watch them walk over to the stadium and take their seats. Wayne told me that it's the only game he gets to all year—and something he looks forward to immensely.

Along with their generosity of spirit and willingness to share both food and recipes, these chefs come to tailgating with the same intensity they take to the kitchen. Alan Wong turns up in the parking lot immaculately dressed, ready to create the best food you ever tasted. Dave Saccomano (Dixie Grill) brings a ton of ribs and enjoys a beer with his crew. And Ryan Day from the Ala Moana Hotel, with his Southern background, is always well prepared; he treats the whole experience like it's the most fun he's had all year. When Philippe Padovani joined us one year, he brought homemade ice cream and portable ovens to keep the food hot. Some of the chefs conduct clinics for anyone who's standing around, and often we have neighboring tailgaters stop by because they can't believe they're watching their favorite chefs cooking in the parking lot. And it's not only chefs who share. Dean Okimoto, the owner of Nalo Farms, often supplies us with his fresh-from-the-field greens, corn and our favorite local tomatoes.

Don Murphy

The grill gets fired up most days at Murphy's Bar and Grill on the corner of Merchant and Nuuanu, where Don Murphy uses a customized smoker that was made for him on the Mainland. If there's anyone who embodies the spirit of UH football and tailgating, it's Don. He's the chairman of Na Koa, the fundraising arm of the football program, and along with his wife Marion he has raised $700,000 at the annual Pigskin Pigout. Monies raised go directly to support the football team via their training table.

It is only fitting, then, that Murph's great tailgating recipes are here. He often teams up with the crew from Gaspro, and together their barbecue skills are second to none. Whether it's lobster tails with shrimp, grilled whole pig, or alligator on a Weber, there's never been a barbecue that Murphy's didn't do well. Amidst the fundraising and tailgating, Murph also manages to find time to run his busy downtown restaurant, where the Honolulu business crowd stops for lunch. His pea salad, featured here, is one of my all-time favorite tailgate dishes. It's a favorite with the UH football coaches, too.

Curried Pea Salad

2-lb. bag	frozen peas
1 cup	chopped green onion
1 cup	sliced water chestnuts
1 cup	thinly sliced celery
1 cup	mayonnaise
1 tbsp.	curry powder, or more to taste

Cook peas in boiling water 10 seconds, then rinse in cold water. Add green onion, water chestnuts and celery. Combine mayonnaise and curry powder. Fold into pea mixture. Chill.

Serves 20

Chipotle-Citrus-Marinated Shrimp

2 lbs.	shrimp, 16-20 count size, peeled, backs split and deveined
	wooden skewers, soaked in water 1 hour

Marinade

1	small can chipotle pepper in adobo sauce (available in Mexican section of grocery stores)
1 qt.	orange juice
2 tbsp.	sesame oil
	sliced fresh citrus fruit (optional)

Chipotle Butter

1 stick	butter, softened
2	chipotle peppers
	adobo sauce, to taste

To make marinade: Grind 4 chipotle peppers and stir into orange juice and sesame oil. Taste and add more if you want it hotter. If using citrus fruit, cut it up and add it to the marinade. Add shrimp to marinade and chill 2 hours. To make chipotle butter: Combine butter with peppers and a small amount of adobo sauce. Prepare a grill. Skewer shrimp through head and out tail. Grill, basting with chipotle butter, until pink.

Serves 12

Murphy's Suckling Pig

1	20-lb. pig (see tips)
1/2 cup	olive oil
10	garlic cloves
1	apple
	sage, parsley and pepper, to taste

Use a sharp knife to poke 6 holes through each ear to allow air to escape. Make a small ball out of foil and place in pig's mouth to hold jaw open. Wash and wipe out inside of pig; dry. Combine olive oil, garlic cloves, sage, parsley and pepper and rub inside pig. Prepare a grill. Lay pig on grill with legs underneath and cook over indirect heat 2-1/2 hours, occasionally rubbing skin with olive oil to make it brown. If pig is too long for grill, curl it around to fit. Put apple in pig's mouth about 1/2 hour before it is done. To check if pig is cooking properly, insert a metal skewer where rear leg and hip meet, all the way to the bone. Pull out. If skewer is cool, pig is not cooking, if warm, it is cooking, if hot, it is doing well, and if very hot, it is done. To serve: Place pig on a serving tray lined with ti leaves. Slice pig through the back, from base of head to tail. Peel the skin on one side toward you. Strip meat from this side and lay next to the side still covered with skin. The largest portion of meat will be under the hindquarter, so gently lift the back side to slice.

| TIPS |

1   Maybe someone at the tailgate is artistic and can carve the UH logo on the skin of the apple.

2   Cooking the pig this way does not usually make for really crispy skin. The pig may be cooked in an oven at home, wrapped in foil and taken to the game.

3   Always get the pig at least two days in advance to make sure it is not too large. Suckling pigs are available in all sizes, up to about 90 pounds. A little will go a long way, so start small.

4   You can order a pig fresh or frozen through Hawaii Food Products or a pork distributor such as HIGA. Allow at least two weeks, to be sure to get the size you need. Order the pig "huli" style, which means the bottom side will be split from throat to groin, not completely split in half.

5   A pig may be cooked in a large Weber kettle or a 55-gallon drum cooker. Smoke chips are optional.

Kalua Pig (or Turkey)

1 4-lb.	pork butt or turkey
4 tbsp.	liquid smoke
1/4 cup	Hawaiian salt

Preheat oven to 300 degrees. Place pork butt or turkey in metal container and add water to fill pan 1-1/2 inches. Sprinkle turkey with liquid smoke and salt. Roast, covered, 8 hours or until meat is easily pulled from bone. (Meat will cook faster at a higher temperature, but slow cooking is better). Drain and reserve most of the juice from the meat. Shred meat, adding back some of the juice if it seems dry.

Variation
To add cabage to meat, core and thinly slice 1/2 a head of cabbage. Bring a pot of water to a boil with 1/2 cup of Hawaiian salt. Boil cabbage 15 seconds, then drain. Combine with shredded meat.

Serves 10-12

| NOTE | *This is also great with Red Bell Pepper Mayonnaise.*

Red Bell Pepper Mayonnaise

1	roasted red bell pepper
2 cups	mayonnaise
2	whole roasted garlic bulbs
	salt and pepper, to taste
	Vietnamese chili sauce, to taste

Pulse all ingredients in food processor. Don't blend too much, or mayonnaise will separate!

Colin Nishida

Colin Nishida is just about the most honest person I know. His cooking has a ton of personality, and he has absolutely no secrets about his food. Ask him how he makes his short ribs taste so good, and he'll fire you over the recipe. Sit down with him late at night at his immensely popular Side Street Bar and Grill, and he'll tell you how he "accidentally" created some of his most popular dishes. He wears slippers and shorts everywhere and has a refreshing air of unpretentiousness in an often-rarified profession.

Leftovers provide inspiration for Colin, and he looks around his kitchen for ideas when a less spontaneous person might search through a recipe book. A piece of pound cake is turned into a dreamy and decadent dessert. Rich, sugary doughnuts go into his bread pudding. And he's elevated humble foods like pork chops with tomato ketchup to cult-like status. There is no chef who comes into town, no matter how famous, who isn't taken to Colin's place for pork chops, and no food writer worthy of the name could visit Honolulu without stopping by Side Street. When Colin comes to tailgate we just know we're in for a treat.

Recreate these recipes and you'll see why he's one of the most popular chefs in Hawai'i—and why Side Street Inn deserves its glowing reputation for food.

Curry-Bacon Potato Salad

6	medium potatoes
1/4 lb.	bacon, diced (may substitute crab meat or imitation crab)
1/4	onion, sliced
1 tsp.	minced garlic
1	shallot, minced
1 tsp.	curry powder
2	hard-boiled eggs, chopped (optional)
1/2 cup	mayonnaise
1 tsp.	Dijon mustard
1/4 cup	chopped green onions
	salt and pepper, to taste

Peel, cube and steam potatoes 10 to 12 minutes or until tender but still firm. Drain and cool in refrigerator 1 hour. Meanwhile, cook bacon until crisp in a pan. Add onions, garlic, shallots and curry powder. Simmer 2 minutes. Add hot mixture to cooled potatoes and mix. Add eggs, mayonnaise, mustard and green onions. Season with salt and pepper.

Serves 8

Hibachi Seafood Mix

1/2 lb.	choy sum
1/2 lb.	baby bok choy (may substitute spinach for baby bok choy and/or choy sum)
2 lb.	snapper (or any other white-fleshed fish), cut into 3-oz. pieces
1 lb.	fresh Manila clams
1/2 lb.	scallops
1/2 lb.	shrimp, cleaned and deveined (may be shelled or not; see note)
1 lb.	shelled king crab legs (optional)
2	lobster tails, 8-oz. each, shelled and meat cubed
1/4 lb.	butter, in pieces
2	lemons, cut into rings
1 tbsp.	minced garlic
1	tomato, diced
1/4 cup	white wine
1/2 cup	clam stock
1/4 cup	chopped tomatoes
	salt, pepper and shoyu, to taste.

Prepare a hibachi. Place clam stock in a 9-by-13-inch foil pan. Place choy sum and bok choy on bottom of pan. Add fish near center and arrange clams and scallops around fish. Place shrimp, crab legs and lobster meat on top of fish. Place butter and lemon rings on top of the seafood. Sprinkle with garlic, tomato, wine and a dash of shoyu. Sprinkle salt and pepper over top. Cover tightly with foil and place on hibachi. Cook until foil puffs up, and then cook an additional 3 to 5 minutes.

Serves 4

NOTE *Shrimp cooked with the shells on taste better, but it's up to you to decide if your guests are going to want to shell them afterward!*

Pulehu Short Ribs

3 lbs.	short ribs, 3/4 inch thick

Marinade

1/4 cup	chili pepper water
2-3 tbsp.	minced garlic
1 tbsp.	fresh-ground black pepper
2 tbsp.	Hawaiian sea salt
1/4 cup	chopped green onions
2 tbsp.	shoyu
1/4 cup	olive oil

Dipping sauce

1/4 cup	chili pepper water
2 tbsp.	shoyu
1 clove	garlic, minced
	chopped green onions, optional

Combine marinade ingredients and pour over short ribs. Let stand 2 hours in refrigerator, turning once. Combine dipping sauce ingredients. Grill ribs and serve with dipping sauce.

Serves 4 to 6

FISH STORIES

Every Saturday afternoon, before we begin broadcasting *The Tailgate Show*, I walk around the parking lot in search of interesting tailgates. Often I stop where I see local guys hunched over a small charcoal grill. They are most often cooking fish—and in most cases, it's fish they caught themselves that morning. This is one of my favorite finds of the day.

You can find almost anything being grilled in the parking lot: Uhu, wahoo, aku, moi. Fresh tako (octopus) is a favorite too, and homemade poke from freshly caught ahi is probably one of the best things you'll taste at a tailgate—or anywhere else! I once had an unbelievably great ahi spread that someone had made by copying the recipe Chef Wayne Hirabayashi uses at Hoku's. Fresh tuna, caught that morning and made into a dip, served with warm baguettes—now, that's the kind of tailgating that makes Hawai'i different.

My favorite tailgates, though, are the ones where the guys are just sitting around a hibachi, drinking beers, worrying seriously about the game and not at all about the food, getting ready to eat the fish they've caught. There's nothing quite like the taste of local fish, simply rubbed with Hawaiian salt and seared on the grill.

Russell Siu

Russell Siu is the chef and co-owner of 3660 On the Rise, the celebrated Asian/Pacific Rim restaurant on Waialae Avenue. He also owns Kaka'ako Kitchen on Ward Avenue. The fact that these two restaurants serve such different food always intrigues me. Russell not only knows fine dining and is one of the best at creating it, he knows the local palate and understands what people want for everyday consumption. He knows when too much sauce is too much, and he knows when we want to ladle it on. His palate is exceptional, as well, which accounts for the extraordinary flavors he puts together at 3660.

When he's tailgating he brings that same passion for excellence, the same quickness of eye and sleight of hand, and the same mesmerizing flavors found in his restaurant food. With Russell the key to good food is, simply, great ingredients and simple preparation. He likes to let the food speak for itself. He started cooking at a local drive-in here on Oahu and was influenced tremendously by his grandparents, who cooked and baked daily.

I love to watch him in the kitchen. He's quick and professional, but he has a wicked sense of humor. I once asked him to help me create a dish to cook at Bali by the Sea. In a matter of minutes he translated what I wanted to do into the dish itself—then made me cook it. I took the recipe to Bali, and we served it that night to none other than President Bill Clinton, who stopped in for dinner and then stopped by the kitchen to say how much he had enjoyed the meal. I always tease Russell that he may have won countless awards for his food—but I've cooked for a president.

Soy Chili Sauce

1 cup	shoyu (Kikkoman or Yamasa preferred)
2 tbsp.	green onions, chopped
1	chili pepper (Hawaiian or Thai), or less, depending on the spiciness you like
2 tbsp.	minced Maui onion
	fresh squeezed lemon juice, to taste

Combine ingredients and let sit for about an hour. If mixture is too salty, dilute with a little water. Use this sauce with oysters, clams or opihi in the shell. Place shellfish on grates over charcoal grill. When shells pop open, take them off the grill and remove top shells. Ladle about a tablespoon of sauce over the meat. Serve immediately.

Grilled Marinated Breast of Chicken with Salsa Verde

6	skinless chicken breasts, 6 oz. each
1/2 tsp.	chopped cilantro
1 tbsp.	chopped fresh sage
1/2 tsp.	chopped garlic
1/4 cup	canola oil
	salt and pepper, to taste
	juice of 1 lime

Salsa Verde

1	tomatillo, peeled, washed and quartered
1	green chili, chopped
1	green onion
1 tbsp.	chopped cilantro
1/3 tsp.	chopped garlic
1 tbsp.	lime juice
	oregano and cumin, to taste
	salt and pepper, to taste

Cut chicken breasts in half. Combine lime juice, cilantro, sage, oil, garlic, salt and pepper. Pour over chicken and toss. Marinate, refrigerated, about 4 hours. To make salsa: In a blender, puree tomatillos, green chili, green onion, cilantro, garlic, lime juice, oregano and cumin. Season with salt and pepper. Taste and add more green chilies if needed to make it spicier. Serve chicken on top of sauce, garnished with more cilantro.

Ti Leaf Shrimp in Foil

1 lb.	shrimp, 16-20 count size, shell on

Marinade

4 tbsp.	chopped garlic
1 tsp.	chopped ginger
1/4 cup	white wine
1/2 cup	softened butter, unsalted
2 tbsp.	chopped parsley
	salt and pepper, to taste

Keeping shells on shrimp, cut them down the backs to pull out veins. Butterfly shrimp by spreading them open and flattening. To make marinade: Combine ingredients in a non-reactive bowl. Add shrimp and marinate 1 hour. Prepare a grill. Place a row of ti leaves on the center of a piece of foil. Place shrimp on ti leaves. Pour some marinade over shrimp and cover again with ti leaves. Fold foil over ti leaves and seal so there are no leaks. Place atop barbecue and grill 5 to 10 minutes.

Sausage and Shrimp Gumbo, Louisiana Style

1/2 cup	flour
2 tsp.	Cajun seasoning
18	shrimp, 21-25 count size, peeled and deveined
1/2 cup	vegetable oil
3/4 lb.	Andouille sausage
1-1/2 cups	diced onion
1 cup	diced green bell pepper
3/4 cup	diced celery
1/4 cup	chopped green onion
1 cup	sliced okra (1/2 inch slices)
1 tbsp.	chopped garlic
1 cup	seafood or chicken stock or clam juice, hot
1	bay leaf
2 tsp.	filé powder.

Mix 2 tbsp. flour with Cajun seasoning. Dry shrimp and toss in seasoned flour. Heat a heavy 3-quart saucepan over medium heat. Add oil and heat 2 to 3 minutes. Quickly sauté shrimp until they just turn pink; remove. Add sausage and stir while cooking, just enough to render some of the fat. Remove. Add remaining flour to oil in the pan and whisk to make a roux. Continue to cook until roux turns dark red or brown. Add vegetables and continue to stir 2 to 3 minutes. Stirring constantly, drizzle stock into roux mixture until stock is incorporated and smooth (make sure stock is hot or roux will bubble and splash). Bring to a boil, and then reduce to simmer. Add bay leaf. When the roux is cooked out (no floury taste remains) return shrimp and sausage to pan. Bring to simmer and cook until shrimp is done. Serve over rice. Remove bay leaf before serving.

Chicken Chili with Three Beans

1/4 cup	dry cannelini beans
1/4 cup	dry cranberry beans
1/4 cup	dry pinto beans
1/2	onion, minced
2 tbsp.	vegetable oil
2 cloves	garlic, minced
1 lb.	ground chicken
3 tbsp.	tomato paste
3 tbsp.	chili powder
1 tbsp.	paprika
1 tbsp.	ground cumin
1/2 tsp.	oregano
3	bay leaves
2	ripe beefsteak tomatoes, diced small
1 cup	canned crushed tomatoes with juice
2 cans	chicken stock
	salt and pepper, to taste

Soak beans in water for 3 hours, then par-boil until tender but not mushy. In a deep skillet or sauce pot, sauté onions in oil about 3 minutes. Add garlic and chicken and sauté until chicken is cooked. Add tomato paste, chili powder, paprika, cumin, oregano and bay leaves. Mix thoroughly over medium heat. Add tomatoes, crushed tomatoes and chicken stock. Simmer about 25 minutes. Add beans and simmer for another 25 minutes. Season with salt and pepper. Remove bay leaf before serving.

| NOTE | *For spicier chili add more chili powder or chopped jalapeno. Serve with flour tortillas or rice.*

ALOHA SPIRITS

At one UH football game during the 2003 season, I encountered Warren Shon, Ron Shinoda, Alan Suzuki and Paul Ah Cook tailgating together. These local guys are, respectively, vice president of Southern Wines and Spirits, regional sales manager for Schieffelin and Somerset, regional sales manager for Robert Mondavi and director of operations for Ruth's Chris Steak House. You can't imagine how well these guys were eating! Dom Perignon, Mondavi wines and Moet et Chandon were in their glasses, and they were cooking the most perfect steak pupu I've ever tasted. Lobster pieces were disappearing off the grill as fast as people could get them into their mouths. I didn't want to leave and do the rest of the show!

Warren Shon is an avid UH supporter who grew up in the Islands. He's also a great cook—and someone who loves to tailgate. To me, Warren personifies the Hawai'i tailgater: Someone who works all week in the corporate world, then spends Friday evening getting ready for a tailgate where the most sophisticated piece of cooking equipment is a hibachi.

During the von Appen years—also known as the "what happened?" years, when coach Fred von Appen's teams lost most of their games—Warren couldn't get anyone to come to the games with him, so he'd sometimes tailgate by himself. He has a very sophisticated palate and knows wine as well as—if not better than—anyone in the state, but his tailgating style is low key: Simple hibachi, grilled steak, fresh fish and homemade pupu. One time he brought a giant glass jar filled with fruit. Layer upon layer of carefully peeled and sliced tropical fruits were soaking in high-quality vodka. The drink was fabulous; the presentation amazing. He'd stayed up most of the night making it.

This group of guys sets the standard for tailgating. And they're all the more special because of their devotion to UH football.

Goran Streng

My friend Vicky came up with the idea that Goran Streng is really the James Bond of chefs here in Hawai'i. He's very debonair, extremely organized, professional, charming, perfectly manicured and always willing to come to your rescue in any food emergency. Any day now, we imagine, he'll parasail into the kitchen at the Hawaii Prince Hotel with not a hair out of place, ready to cook a banquet for thousands.

Naturally, it goes without saying that he's a terrific chef—with a good sense of humor. He's the executive chef at the Hawaii Prince, and he's a tremendous supporter of local farmers and their products. Every year when everyone else is getting nervous about Thanksgiving, he calmly organizes thousands of pounds of "turkeys to go." He's been a guest on my radio show for the past five or six Thanksgivings, and every year he answers the same questions about cooking a perfect turkey with grace and patience. I'm sure many people owe their successful dinners to his tips.

He's a very easy chef to work with, and his food is always something I look forward to tasting. His recipes, matched with his unflappable attitude, make him an excellent choice for tailgating. Here are five recipes that you can make at home and take anywhere.

Ahi Cakes with Roasted Sweet Corn Relish

1 lb.	fresh ahi, finely chopped
1/2 cup	diced onion
1/4 cup	finely sliced green onion
2 tbsp.	chopped cilantro
2 tsp.	sambal olek (Thai chili-garlic sauce)
2 tsp.	lime juice
2 tbsp.	Worcestershire sauce
	salt and pepper, to taste
	vegetable oil for pan-frying, about 1 tbsp.

Sweet Corn Relish

2 ears	sweet corn, roasted
1 cup	diced papaya
1/4 cup	diced red bell pepper
1/4 cup	diced green bell pepper
1/4 cup	diced sweet onion
1/4 cup	balsamic vinegar
1/2 cup	olive oil
2 tbsp.	cilantro
	salt and pepper, to taste

To make ahi cakes: Combine all ingredients except oil in a bowl and mix well. Heat oil in a sauté pan. Use a small ice cream scoop to spoon mix directly into pan. Cook about 1 minute per side. To make relish: Cut corn off cob and combine with other ingredients. Serve cakes hot with relish.

Serves 6

Sesame-Hoisin-Glazed Lamb Chops

16	small lamb chops

Hoisin Barbecue Sauce

1 slice	bacon, diced
2 tbsp.	diced onion
1 tsp.	chopped garlic
1/2 tsp.	minced ginger
1/2 tsp.	minced lemongrass, optional
1 pinch	fresh thyme
1 pinch	black pepper
1/4 tsp.	Chinese five-spice
1/4 cup	red wine vinegar
1/4 cup	plum wine
1/2 tbsp.	sesame oil
1 piece	star anise (optional)
1/4 cup	plum sauce
1/4 cup	hoisin sauce
1 tbsp.	kecap manis (sweet soy sauce)
1/2 cup	ketchup
1/2 tbsp.	brown sugar

To make hoisin barbecue sauce: Sauté bacon and add onion. Cook until light brown. Add garlic, ginger and lemongrass. Add thyme, pepper and five-spice. Deglaze pan with vinegar. Reduce until almost dry. Turn off the heat and add all remaining ingredients to the bacon-onion mixture. Let sauce cool to room temperature. Marinate chops in hoisin barbecue sauce for 1 hour. Cook on grill until medium rare, about 2 minutes per side.

Serves 4

Oriental Chicken Salad

1/2 head	iceberg or romaine lettuce, chopped
1/2 head	won bok, chopped
1 cup	bean sprouts
1/2 cup	snow peas or snap peas, blanched
1/2 cup	red bell pepper, cut in fine strips
1/2 cup	green bell pepper, cut in fine strips
1/2 cup	carrots, cut in fine sticks
2 cups	thinly sliced grilled chicken breast, or shredded chicken thigh (may substitute 1 whole roasted chicken or duck, shredded)
	fried won ton pi strips, for garnish

Dressing

3/4 cup	hoisin sauce
1/3 cup	sesame oil
3/4 cup	salad oil
1/3 cup	white wine vinegar
2 tbsp.	sugar
1/4 tsp.	dry mustard
1 pinch	white pepper

Combine dressing ingredients and blend well. Combine vegetables and chicken; toss with dressing. Garnish with won ton pi.

Serves 4, amply

Stir-Fried Noodles

2 tbsp.	peanut oil
1 tbsp.	sesame oil
2 tbsp.	ginger, finely julienned
2 tsp.	minced garlic
1	carrot, julienned
2 stalks	celery, julienned
1/2	onion, julienned
2	green onions, julienned
1 cup	thinly sliced char siu pork
1 lb.	chow mein noodles
1/2 cup	chicken stock
2 tbsp.	oyster sauce
4 tbsp.	shoyu
1 tsp.	chili paste

Heat peanut and sesame oils in a wok. Stir-fry ginger, garlic and vegetables quickly. Keep crisp. Add char siu and noodles; mix well. Add stock, oyster sauce, shoyu and chili paste. Stir and toss ingredients until liquids reduce and mixture is almost dry. Serve hot.

Serves 8

Chocolate Macadamia Nut Pie

Crust

1-1/4 cups	flour
1 tbsp.	sugar
1/2 tsp.	salt
1 stick	cold unsalted butter, cut into 1/2-inch pieces
2 tbsp.	ice water

Filling

3/4 cup	sugar
1 stick	butter
1/3 cup	cream
1 cup	diced macadamia nuts

Topping

1-1/4 cups	heavy cream
3-1/2 oz.	chocolate, melted and cooled (1 premium chocolate bar or a generous 1/2 cup of chocolate chips)

To make crust: Combine flour, sugar and salt in a food processor and pulse to blend. Add butter gradually and pulse until mixture forms grains the size of peas. Add ice water and process just until dough comes together. Flatten dough slightly into a disk, wrap it in plastic and refrigerate 1 hour. Preheat oven to 400 degrees. Press dough into a 9-inch fluted pie tin—no need to roll it out. Trim edges and prick bottom several times with a fork. Line pie shell with foil and fill with pie weights or dried beans to keep crust from puffing up. Bake 10 minutes. Carefully remove shell from oven and remove foil and weights. Bake shell 20 minutes longer, until golden brown. Cool completely on wire rack. To make filling: Brown sugar in a pan to caramelize. (It will happen—just be patient! Be careful not to burn it.) Add butter and cream; stir in nuts. Cool to room temperature and then pour into pie shell. Place in refrigerator until it's set enough to spread topping on. To make topping: Whip cream and add melted chocolate. Spread on top of filling. Chill overnight before serving.

Makes 1 pie

Alan Wong

Alan Wong is one of the most creative and inspired chefs in Hawai'i. At his restaurants, Alan Wong's on South King Street and The Pineapple Room in Ala Moana, he delivers dishes that leave you almost speechless. He has a Zen-like approach to his work, and I've always thought that part of his creativity is that he doesn't think like the rest of us. He looks at food differently. When you interview him, he pauses before answering questions and really ponders what he wants to say. Not because he has to, but because, I think, he wants people to understand him in a clear and simple way. He does something that is mysterious with food, but he's anxious to take the mystery away from it. He loves sports, and he always uses sporting analogies when he's interviewing potential employees. He says it gives him a good idea of how they think and how they'd work in a team.

When we first asked him to tailgate with us, I was a little nervous as I drove out to meet him in the parking lot. That didn't last long, though. One of the dishes he recreated for us the first year was the "Opihi Bag," which appears on page 90. I remember watching him unwrap pieces of foil and thinking that the flavors emanating from the pouches were intoxicating. People really couldn't believe how good the seafood tasted and yet how simple it all seemed. This year he created a whole-tomato salad with a li hing mui vinaigrette that was as beautiful as it was delicious. For Alan's recipes, use the best possible ingredients you can find. On O'ahu, try the farmer's market at Kapi'olani Community College for the fresh produce and other local ingredients.

This is tailgating for those of you who want to make a statement, a simple one: Work at excellence.

Asian Guacamole

2	avocadoes, peeled, pitted and diced
1/2 cup	diced onions
1/2 cup	diced tomatoes
3 tbsp	sake
1/4 cup.	sliced green onions, green parts only
2 tbsp.	freshly squeezed lime juice
2 tbsp.	minced ginger
1 tbsp.	chopped cilantro
1 tbsp.	vegetable oil
1/2 tsp.	chili-garlic sauce (such as sambal olek)
1 tsp.	chili pepper water
1 tsp.	salt

Combine all ingredients in a bowl. Mix gently without mashing the avocadoes. Serve immediately, or cover with plastic wrap and refrigerate up to 2 days.

Makes 4 to 5 cups

Barbecue Ribs

5 lbs.	pork ribs (2 racks)

Sauce

1-1/2 cups	hoisin sauce (see note)
1/2 cup	plum sauce (see note)
1 tbsp.	siracha (Thai chili sauce)
2 tbsp.	garlic black bean sauce (see note)
1 tbsp.	honey
1 tbsp.	sugar
1 tbsp.	brown sugar
1/2 tsp.	ginger
1/2 tsp.	garlic
1/4 cup	freshly squeezed orange juice
1 tsp.	sesame oil

Grill ribs over fire until firm (or well done). Preheat oven to 500 degrees. Place ribs in a large braising pan filled with about 2 inches of water. Braise in oven about 2 hours. Almost all the water will evaporate, but do not allow the pan to burn. Meanwhile, make the sauce: Combine the ingredients in a large bowl and mix evenly. Set aside. Place cooked ribs on a sheet pan and cool to room temperature. Baste with sauce. Reserve any extra sauce. To reheat the ribs, place in a 500-degree oven and baste with reserved sauce twice while heating. The ribs should have a nice, shiny glaze.

Serves 2 to 4

| NOTE | *Recommended brand for all three sauces is Kuoon Chun Sauce Factory.*

Opihi Bag

1 tbsp.	butter
2 tsp.	minced garlic
1/2 cup	quartered shiitake mushrooms
2 cups	firmly packed spinach
	opihi, desired amount
8	shrimp, peeled and deveined
1	Portuguese sausage, sliced
2	lobster tails
20	Manila clams, washed
2 cups	kalua pig
1 cup	finely diced tomatoes
4 cups	chicken stock
4 cups	water

Prepare the grill. Cut a strip of 18-inch-wide, heavy-duty foil 60 inches long (or use 2 overlapping strips of 12-inch-wide foil). Cut the foil into 4 equal lengths. Form 4 foil bags by folding each strip of foil in half lengthwise, then folding the side edges over 3 or 4 times. Leave one end of each bag open. In a sauté pan over medium-high heat, melt butter. Add garlic and sauté for 2 minutes, stirring occasionally. Add mushrooms and sauté for 2 more minutes. Blanch spinach for 30 seconds in boiling water. Transfer to an ice bath to cool. Drain and gently squeeze out any excess moisture. For each serving, combine in a large ovenproof soup bowl opihi, shrimp, sausage, lobster tail, mushrooms, spinach, clams, kalua pig and tomatoes. Pour 1 cup of chicken stock into the bowl. Slide the bowl into the foil bag. Pour 1 cup warm water into the bag, and then seal the open end. Carefully place the bags on the grill. Close the lid of the grill and heat 15 minutes. The steam created by the water inside the bags will puff up the foil and cook the ingredients inside. If a bag does not puff up, check for holes or leaks. To serve, place each bag on a large plate. Cut open at the table. Be careful, as hot steam will rise from the bag. Discard any clams that do not open during cooking.

Serves 4

Tableside Poke

1/2 tsp.	soy-mustard sauce (shoyu and hot mustard mixed)
1/2 tsp.	sambal olek sauce
1/2 tsp.	minced onion
1/4 tsp.	chopped ogo
2	shiso leaves
2 tbsp.	ikura (salmon eggs)
3 oz.	ahi, cut in 1/4-inch cubes
1 pinch	inamona (ground kukui nut)
1 pinch	chopped chives
1	opihi
2 slices	tako (octopus)
1 piece	uni (sea urchin)
1/4 tsp.	wasabi tobiko (wasabi-flavored flying fish roe) (see note)
1/4 tsp.	tobiko (flying fish roe)
1/4 tsp.	yuzu tobiko (flying fish roe flavored with Japanese citrus) (see note)

Use at least a 10-inch rectangular plate. Thinly line soy-mustard sauce horizontally across the top portion of the plate. Evenly space the sambal, onions and ogo on top of the mustard sauce, in separate mounds. Top each shiso leaf with a tablespoon of ikura. In the middle of the plate, below the line of soy mustard sauce, line up 1 shiso leaf, the ahi (spread out horizontally) and the second shiso leaf. Sprinkle the ahi with inamona and chives. Line up 3 teaspoons on top of the ahi. The bowls of the spoons should rest on the ahi; the handles should rest on the top rim of the plate, alternating with the mounds sambal, onions and ogo. Fill the spoons with opihi, tako and uni. On the bottom of the plate, squirt or thinly line more soy-mustard sauce. Sprinkle with wasabi tobiko, yuzu tobiko and tobiko.

Serves 1 to 2

| NOTE | *Wasabi tobiko and yuzu tobiko can be purchased at Asian food stores, or at the Cherry Company.*

Roy Yamaguchi

Roy Yamaguchi really needs no introduction. He is Hawai'i's most famous chef: He has more than 30 restaurants worldwide, yet he still finds time to take part in local fundraisers, cook at his flagship restaurant—Roy's Hawaii Kai—when he's in town, and run some of the most professional restaurants in the Islands. His team of sous chefs, wait-staff and sommeliers is second to none, and the whole Roy's experience is always of the highest standard. In June a much-anticipated new Roy's opened out at Ko Olina, bringing a new era of fine dining to the West side of Oahu.

But when it comes down to it, Roy Yamaguchi loves to barbecue as much as the next guy, and he's happy cooking out with his friends on the rare occasions they're all in town at the same time. He uses a kamado at home and relishes the time he has with friends, family and good food. "Nothing tastes better than food that's cooked outside," he says. Nothing does—as long as he's cooking.

He is as generous as he is talented, and I've always found him incredibly willing to share time, recipes and ideas. He does, however, have the most serious expression of any of the chefs I've interviewed. The first time I interviewed him for the radio I thought I'd never seen such a stern-looking chef. Then he beamed that famous Roy Yamaguchi smile, seen by millions on his highly successful PBS program *Hawaii Cooks*. Here are three recipes that are typically Roy. Two are so simple you'll do them in minutes; the other needs—but rewards!—patience and attention to detail.

Roy's Baby Back Ribs

2-lb. slab	pork baby back ribs
2 tbsp.	garlic powder
1-1/2 tsp.	finely ground white pepper
2-1/2 tsp.	kosher salt
1/2 cup	red wine vinegar
3/4 cup	butter, melted and cooled

Sprinkle ribs with garlic powder, pepper and salt. Place in a flat pan or sealable plastic bag. Add vinegar, coating the ribs well. Pour butter over ribs and mix well. Marinate 2 to 3 hours at room temperature. Heat a covered charcoal or gas grill to medium heat. Place ribs on grill, meat side down. Cover and cook slowly, checking to be sure ribs do not burn. Baste with remaining marinade a few times. When ribs are nicely browned, turn. Continue to cook, for a total of about 30 minutes. Remove ribs from grill, place on platter and cover with foil. Allow to rest 30 minutes before slicing into individual riblets and serving.

Serves 4 as an appetizer

Shrimp Barbecue

3 lbs.	shrimp (16-20 count size)
1/4 cup	minced garlic
1/2 cup	shoyu
1/2 lb.	unsalted butter, melted

Combine all ingredients in sealable plastic bag. Refrigerate overnight. Once at the tailgate party, grill shrimp to desired doneness.

Shrimp on a Sugar Cane Stick with Pineapple-Mango Jam

3/4 lb.	uncooked mung bean noodles
1 tbsp.	uncooked white rice
16	shrimp (about 1/2 lb.) peeled, deveined and tails removed
4 oz.	minced pork with fat, about 1/2 cup
3 strips	bacon, minced
4	water chestnuts
1/2 tsp.	salt
2 tsp.	sugar
1 tbsp.	fish sauce
2 tbsp.	garlic oil (see note)
12	sugar cane sticks, 3 inches long and 1/4-inch thick
	peanut oil, for deep frying
	lettuce leaves, for garnish

Pineapple-Mango Jam

1 cup	finely diced fresh pineapple
1 cup	finely diced ripe mango
2-3 tbsp.	sugar
1 cup	sweet white wine or sake

To prepare jam: Combine pineapple, mango, sugar and wine in a saucepan over high heat. Bring to a boil, and then decrease heat to low and simmer 30 to 45 minutes, until thick and reduced by half. Place noodles in a large paper bag and break to separate them (the bag keeps pieces from scattering). Bring 2 cups of water to a boil and add noodles. Cook 3 minutes, or until tender. Drain and rinse under cool water. Make a toasted rice powder by toasting rice in a small pan over medium high heat 3 to 4 minutes, shaking pan occasionally, until golden brown. Cool. Grind to a powder in a spice grinder. Place half the shrimp in a food processor and chop to fine mince. Add remaining shrimp, pork, bacon, water chestnuts, noodles, salt, sugar, fish sauce, rice powder and garlic oil. Process until the mixture is pasty but the shrimp is still a little chunky. Moisten hands with water and shape 1/4 cup of shrimp mixture in a ball around the middle of a sugar-cane stick. Repeat to make 12 sticks. Sticks may be refrigerated, covered, several hours before frying. Pour oil into a wok to a depth of 3-4 inches. Heat oil over high heat, and then decrease heat to medium-high. Slide shrimp sticks in, 2 or 3 at a time. Fry 3 to 5 minutes, turning, until golden brown. Transfer to paper towels to drain excess oil. Line a serving platter with lettuce leaves. Arrange shrimp sticks on leaves and serve immediately, with jam on the side.

Serves 6

| NOTE | *To make garlic oil, heat 1/4 cup vegetable oil over medium heat, then add 2 tbsp. minced garlic. Cook 2 minutes, stirring every 30 seconds, until garlic just begins to turn color. Remove from the heat and let steep until cool. Strain. Oil may be stored, covered, in refrigerator for up to 3 days. Cooked garlic may be saved for other uses. Makes 1/4 cup garlic oil.*

Recipe courtesy of Ten Speed Press from the cookbook Hawaii Cooks, Flavors from Roy's Pacific Rim Kitchen, *a companion cookbook to the public television series* Hawaii Cooks with Roy Yamaguchi.

Mixed Plate

Everything I learned about tailgating on a grand scale I owe to the gang at Gaspro, the century-old company that sells industrial gases, medical equipment and thousands of other products—including, of course, state-of-the-art grills. They're also the most professional group of tailgaters you'll ever meet. They not only host the largest tailgate party in Hawai'i, they can often be found "wokking" and deep-frying turkeys at fundraisers around the Islands.

It helps, of course, that they have some of the best equipment money can buy. Weber grills and King Cookers for deep-fat frying certainly help to make the whole process a lot easier. But it's not just the equipment. These folks have a commitment to doing things well. They're at Aloha Stadium early on game mornings, waiting in line with every other football fan and food enthusiast. They're organized and they all love the fun of tailgating. Oh, and did I mention that they're all season-ticket holders and passionate UH supporters? For me, it just wouldn't be tailgating without Margie Yoshioka (opposite), George, John the bartender, Richard, and the rest of the gang at their incredible tailgates. They've served everything from lobster tails to stir-fried noodles with fresh Kaua'i shrimp. Their most popular dish, though, is their expertly deep-fried turkey. (You'll find the recipe for that on page 106.) Nothing tastes as good as that tender moist meat, eaten hot with a serving of mashed potatoes or rice.

On the following pages are a few of Gaspro's most popular recipes, as well as a couple of my own. Enjoy!

Jammin' Jim's Jambalaya

6 strips	bacon, diced
1 lb.	Portuguese sausage
1 lb.	smoked sausage
2	large onions, chopped
1	large green pepper, chopped
8 cloves	garlic, minced
2 lbs.	chicken drumettes (optional)
8 cups	chicken stock (1/2 cup more if you want moist jambalaya)
3 tbsp.	Kitchen Bouquet Browning and Seasoning Sauce
	mushrooms, sliced
1/2 lb.	green onions, minced
1 cup	bay leaves
3	Uncle Ben's Converted Rice (1 box)
2 lbs.	salt, black pepper, cayenne pepper and parsley, to taste

Fry bacon in a pot. Add sausages and cook until done. Remove from pot. Pour off all but an inch of the fat; add onions and bell peppers; cook 3 minutes. Add garlic and cook until vegetables are tender; remove from pot. If using chicken, strip the meat from the bones, season with salt and red pepper, and stir-fry in same pot until brown. Remove from pot. Bring chicken stock and Kitchen Bouquet to boil in pot. Season lightly with salt, pepper and cayenne (or use King Kooker Cajun Seasoning). When seasoning, keep in mind that jambalaya will turn out spicier and saltier than the stock. Add sausage mixture, chicken, mushrooms, parsley, green onions, bay leaves and rice. Bring to a boil again, stirring constantly. Reduce heat to low and simmer, covered, 20 minutes. Stir. Re-cover and let stand minutes. Remove bay leaves before serving.

Serves a crowd!

Hawaiian-Style Seafood Boil

8 qts.	water
1 cup	Hawaiian salt
1 cup	chili pepper water
1 bag	Crab Boil (available at Gaspro)
3	large Maui onions, halved width-wise
2 lbs.	new potatoes
6	garlic cloves, halved width-wise
6	lemons, halved
2 lbs.	Portuguese sausage (optional)
3 lbs.	large Kahuku shrimp
2	large Dungeness crabs, cleaned (optional)
1 lb.	mushrooms
8 ears	corn

Bring water to a boil. Add salt, chili pepper water and crab boil. Add onions, potatoes, garlic and lemons, plus sausage, if using. Boil 20 minutes. Add shrimp, crab, mushrooms and corn. Return to boil and cook 5 minutes. Make sure everything is still covered by water and let sit 10 minutes. Drain. Serve over butcher paper or newspaper with ice-cold drinks.

Serves a bunch!

Chicken and Lobster Stir-Fry on Fried Chinese Cake Noodles

1 lb.	chicken thighs, skinned, deboned and diced
1 tbsp.	minced ginger
1 tbsp.	minced garlic
2 tbsp.	vegetable oil
1 cup	straw mushrooms
1/2 lb.	sugar snap peas, cleaned
1-1/2 cups	chicken stock
3 tbsp.	oyster sauce
1 tsp.	sugar
2 tbsp.	cornstarch
1/2 lb.	cooked lobster meat or imitation crab meat
	salt and white pepper, to taste.

Cake Noodles

3 tbsp.	vegetable oil
2 lbs.	cooked saimin-style noodles

To make noodles: Heat oil in a pan. When hot, add noodles and press down hard. Fry noodles like a pancake until golden brown on both sides. Set aside. Season chicken with salt and white pepper. Stir-fry ginger and garlic in oil. Add chicken and cook until brown. Add mushrooms and peas. Add 1/2 cup chicken stock, oyster sauce and sugar. Mix cornstarch with remaining 1 cup chicken broth; add to pot. Cook until mixture begins to thicken, then add lobster. When lobster is heated through, serve over noodles.

Serves 4-6

Mom's Recipe for Crab with Black Bean Sauce

4 tbsp.	Chinese black beans
6 cloves	garlic, grated
2 tbsp.	vegetable oil
3 tbsp.	oyster sauce
2 tbsp	shoyu
1 tbsp.	chili pepper flakes
1 cup	chicken stock
	cornstarch, as needed (start with 1 tsp.), dissolved in water
2	large Dungeness crabs, cooked and cleaned
	Chinese parsley and chopped green onions, for garnish

Soak black beans in water 30 minutes; drain. Coarsely chop beans and add garlic. Sauté mixture in oil. Add oyster sauce, shoyu and chili flakes. Add chicken stock and thicken with mixture of cornstarch slurry. Add crab and cook until heated through. Garnish with Chinese parsley and chopped green onions.

Serves 2

Deep-Fried Turkey

1	12-lb. turkey
3-1/2 gal.	peanut oil

Cajun Seasoning

4 tbsp.	salt
2 tbsp.	garlic powder
4 tsp.	onion powder
2 tsp.	black pepper
2 tsp.	ground green onion
2 tsp.	cayenne pepper

First use turkey to determine proper oil level (see Safety Tip 5). Rub turkey inside and out with some of the oil. Combine seasoning ingredients and rub over turkey. Refrigerate at least 2 hours or overnight (better) to seal in juices. Heat peanut oil in a turkey fryer to 350 degrees. Place turkey on turkey rack and slowly lower into hot oil. Maintain temperature at 325 to 350 degrees. Cook 3-1/2 to 4 minutes per pound.

Serves everyone who's been looking on with fear and envy

| NOTE | *This recipe may be used for chicken, though it's not as dramatic. Chicken cooks at 7–1/2 minutes per pound.*

| SAFETY TIPS |

1 | Wear personal protective equipment—gloves, eye goggles, shoes (not slippers).

2 | Use thermometer to check oil temperature (no higher than 350 degrees); attend burner and pot at all times.

3 | Use a burner with a pot-retaining ring.

4 | Turn off burner before removing turkey.

5 | To keep oil from spilling over, determine the proper oil level by first doing this trial run: Put turkey in pot, then fill pot with water to at least 4 inches below lip of pot. Remove turkey, and then mark the pot at water level. This mark is where you should fill the pot with oil to. Make sure you dry pot and turkey well before adding oil.

6 | To reduce intense oil bubbling, thaw out turkey completely before submerging.

7 | Do not use animal-fat oil for frying; use vegetable, peanut or cottonseed. Animal-fat oil overheats quickly once turkey is removed.

Baby Back Pork Ribs

3 slabs	lean, meaty baby back pork ribs
1 can	beer
	Hawaiian salt and pepper, to taste
	Cajun seasoning, to taste
	prepared barbecue sauce, tangy style

Prepare a grill. Season ribs with salt, pepper and Cajun seasoning. Place on 2 layers of heavy foil (enough to wrap around the ribs). Pour beer over ribs, and then seal foil tightly. Cook ribs on a grill over indirect/medium heat (275 degrees) for 2 hours. Remove ribs from foil and place directly on grill for 20 minutes, basting frequently with barbecue sauce.

Serves 3

Garlic-Herb Bread

16 oz. loaf	French or Italian bread
1 clove	garlic, crushed
1/4 cup	softened butter or margarine
1/4 tsp. each	dried basil and oregano, crushed
1/4 cup	grated Parmesan cheese
	pepper and salt, to taste

Prepare grill. Cut bread into 1-inch slices without cutting through bottom crust. Mix butter with garlic and spices. Spread cut surfaces with butter mixture and sprinkle with cheese. Wrap loaf in heavy foil; seal with double fold on top and ends. Place bread in center of grate on a grill over indirect/medium heat and heat 15 to 20 minutes or until heated through. For a crisp crust, loosen foil on top and ends for last 5 minutes of heating time.

Salmon Skewers

2 lbs.	skinless salmon fillets
2	lemons, sliced
	sprigs of fresh parsley or dill and lemon wedges, for garnish

Marinade

1/2 cup	chopped fresh dill or 2 tsp. dried dill
2 tbsp.	Pernod or other anise-flavored liqueur, or brandy
1/2 tsp.	seasoned salt
1/2 tsp.	freshly ground pepper

Cut salmon into strips 1 inch wide and 3 inches long. Combine marinade ingredients in a large bowl. Add salmon and toss to combine. Cover and refrigerate 2 hours, tossing once or twice. Prepare grill. Remove salmon from marinade, reserving marinade. Thread salmon strips onto skewers, weaving each strip so that skewer passes through it two or three times. Skewer lemon slices between salmon pieces. Arrange skewers on grill rack. Grill, turning frequently and brushing with reserved marinade, until salmon is cooked through, 8 to 10 minutes. Remove to a warmed platter and garnish with parsley or dill and lemon wedges.

Serves 4

| NOTE | *The best cut for these skewers is a skinned and filleted salmon tail, which has few bones.*

Stuffed Bell Peppers

6 oz.	brown-and-wild rice mix or Uncle Ben's Rice
1/2 cup	coarsely chopped pecans
2 tbsp.	sliced green onions, white and green parts
2 tbsp.	butter
4	bell peppers
4 oz.	mushrooms, sliced
	grated rind of 1 small orange
	grated rind of 1 small lemon
	white pepper, to taste

Prepare rice with water and salt according to package directions. Do not use spice packet. Sauté pecans and green onions in butter in small skillet until pecans are toasted; stir in mushrooms and cook 2 minutes. Combine pecan mixture with rice; stir in orange and lemon rind. Season to taste with white pepper. Cut the stems off the bell peppers and scrape out white membrane and seeds. If desired, lay the peppers on the grill just long enough to blacken the skins. Spoon stuffing into peppers with fork, wrap loosely in foil and cook 50 to 60 minutes.

Serves 4

Shrimp Kabobs

1 lb.	shrimp, peeled and deveined
1 lb.	mushrooms
2	bell peppers (red, green or yellow)
1	large onion
2 ears	corn
	mayonnaise, to taste
	Cajun seasoning, to taste

Cut corn ears into slices about an inch thick. Arrange shrimp, mushroom, peppers, onion and corn pieces alternately on 4 metal skewers. Baste with mayonnaise and sprinkle with Cajun seasoning. Refrigerate 1 hour. Prepare grill. Place kabobs in center of lightly greased cooking grate. Cook until shrimp turns pink, 8 to 10 minutes, turning halfway through cooking time

Serves 4

Down-and-Dirty Rice

1 lb.	bacon, chopped
1	Maui onion, chopped
1 bunch	green onions, chopped
1	green pepper, chopped
1 lb.	mushrooms, chopped
10 cups	cooked rice, refrigerated overnight
1/2 cup	soy sauce, or more to taste
1/4 cup	oyster sauce, or more to taste
1 tbsp.	Kitchen Bouquet Browning and Seasoning Sauce
2	eggs, beaten

Cook bacon in wok until browned. Add onions and cook until tender. Add green peppers and mushrooms. Continue cooking. Add rice, tossing with vegetables. Season with soy sauce, oyster sauce and Kitchen Bouquet. Add eggs and continue tossing until eggs are cooked through.

Serves a crowd!

Jo's Serious Guacamole

4	locally grown tomatoes (Hau'ula, if you can find them)
4	ripe, locally grown avocados
2	shallots (or 1/2 medium onion), chopped
2	garlic cloves, crushed
	juice of 1 lime
3	fresh red chilies, minced (or 2 tsp. dried red pepper flakes)
1	bunch cilantro, chopped
dash	cumin (optional)
	salt, to taste

Cut an X into the bottom of each tomato. Cover with boiling water and let sit a few minutes to loosen skins. Lift tomatoes carefully and plunge into a bowl of iced water. Drain. The skins will have begun to peel back. Remove skins and squeeze out seeds. Roughly chop flesh and set aside. Halve avocados, remove pits with a spoon or sharp knife, and scoop out flesh. Mash vigorously with a fork or purée in a food processor. (I prefer the texture created by hand, but if you prefer a smoother taste, the food processor is best.) Put shallots or onion, garlic and lime juice into a bowl and add avocado. Add chilies or pepper flakes and tomatoes to bowl. Add cilantro and mix well. Add cumin and salt. Cover immediately and refrigerate until ready to serve.

| NOTE | *Guacamole is perhaps the most popular way to enjoy an avocado. Even at the most sophisticated tailgate, you can be sure someone will still bring chips and dip. And if that dip is guacamole, the contributor will be welcomed with open arms.*

Jo's Spicy Beef Brochettes

1	large onion, diced
3	cloves garlic, roughly chopped
1	small red chili, seeds removed and cut into strips
1-1/2 lbs.	ground beef
1 tbsp.	red pepper flakes
1	bunch fresh parsley
1	bunch fresh cilantro
1/2 tsp.	dried oregano
1 tsp.	paprika
2 tsp.	ground cumin
	salt and black pepper, to taste
	Rosemary sticks or lemongrass stalks, optional

Garnish
plain yogurt
cucumber, diced
green onions, minced

Place onion, garlic and chili in food processor; blend. Add ground beef, pepper flakes, herbs, spices, salt and pepper and blend until combined. Transfer to a non-reactive bowl. Cover and refrigerate for at least an hour. Meanwhile, soak wooden skewers in water. Mold meat mixture into sausage shapes around skewers. If you like, add rosemary or lemongrass sticks to make a double skewer, with ends of rosemary or lemongrass visible. (Do not use rosemary alone, as the meat will probably fall off.) Grill brochettes over a hot grill or coals about 6 minutes, turning frequently. Combine yogurt with cucumber and onion and drizzle over brochettes. Serve hot.

| NOTE | *This recipe is quick, simple and easy to eat. It takes boring hamburger ingredients and gives people a reason to rave about them. The rosemary sticks or lemongrass stalks add extra flavor.*

TAILGATING TIPS

Grilling Veggies

There's almost no other way to make vegetables taste as good as they do straight from the grill. Flavors are intensified and color remains bright, adding extra zip to your tailgate menu. The two easiest ways to grill veggies are in foil packets and, marinated, directly over the heat.

For foil packet steaming, make sure the veggies are all cut to roughly the same size and will need approximately the same cooking time (e.g., don't put red peppers and potatoes in the same packet). Assemble the veggies and place them on a thick layer of foil. Add a couple of tablespoons of water, a dollop of butter, salt, pepper, and additional seasoning if desired. Fold the corners of the foil together to make a packet and grill over medium heat for 8 to 10 minutes. Carefully remove and open packets—they will be hot! And that's all it takes for perfectly steamed veggies.

To marinate and then grill veggies over direct heat, choose ones with similar consistency and cooking time—yellow squash, zucchini, red peppers, asparagus and eggplant are good examples. Slice them to about 1/4" thick and marinate them for an hour or more in your favorite liquid. Place on grill over medium-high heat, turning several times, until they are slightly charred. Serve immediately—sprinkled with goat cheese for added flavor.

How High?

Remember, there's a difference between high heat and low heat. High heat with lots of flame will burn and char your food. Medium heat and low flame will give sweetness and a moister end result. Barbecue is about taking the time to get the best from food.

How Long?

Make sure you understand exactly how long you need to cook meats, poultry or fish. Overcooking is one of the easiest mistakes to avoid: You just need an idea of how long food should take. Remember, fish will continue to cook after it has been removed from heat, so don't be afraid to slightly undercook fish on the grill and then leave it to sit a few minutes. Chicken, on the other hand, needs to be cooked thoroughly—no red juices should remain when the chicken is done. To test steaks, press the meat with your index finger and judge according to the resistance you feel. Soft, spongy meat is still raw, firmer meat is medium, and meat that is almost firm to the touch is well done.

Marinades

One of the easiest ways to achieve grilling perfection is to marinate meats, fish and poultry before you begin. Marinades add flavor and moisture and can significantly ease the cooking process. Oils, vinegars, lemon juice and wine are all useful as bases. Add fresh or dried herbs, chilies and spices to bring flavor to the marinade. Plain yogurt is a wonderful base for a chicken marinade, as it serves to both tenderize and moisten the meat. Add chopped garlic, turmeric, lemon juice, chili powder and curry powder, and you have a wonderful spicy marinade that will add flavor and also help the chicken cook faster.

Papaya enzymes are good for tenderizing—but don't leave the meat in these marinades too long, as it will become mushy. Salt creates the opposite problem—don't add it to a marinade until you're ready to cook. It draws out moisture, leaving the meat tough and tasteless.

Sweet marinades bring more than just added flavor; they cause meats to brown and crisp better, giving a rich, caramelized look to the finished product. Honey, molasses and concentrated fruit juice all work well.

Index

About the Author

Jo McGarry was born in St. Andrews, Scotland, with a view of the Royal and Ancient Golf Course. She lived and worked in Edinburgh and traveled the world—sampling the local foods of many cultures—before moving to Hawai'i, where she has been writing about food and wine since the 1990s. Previously editor of *Gusto Magazine*, Jo began working as restaurant specialist for the *Honolulu Star-Bulletin* in 2001 and writing a food column for *MidWeek* the same year. Today, her columns reach more than 400,000 people each week. She also hosts *Table Talk*, the long-running lunchtime lifestyle program on KKEA 1420 AM. Because local Island produce is one of Jo's passions, her Tuesday radio show has, since 1998, been devoted exclusively to promoting local farmers. Her co-host is Dean Okimoto. She is a freelance writer, a musician, a single malt scotch enthusiast and a mom. She is also known as "the voice of tailgating"—bringing the pre-game tailgate show to thousands of devoted University of Hawai'i fans during football season. Jo is married to sportscaster Bobby Curran.

SHARE
THE HAWAI'I
TAILGATE
COOKBOOK
WITH FAMILY AND
FRIENDS!

Watermark Publishing
1088 Bishop Street, Suite 310
Honolulu, Hawaii 96813

Toll-free 1-866-900-BOOK
sales@bookshawaii.net

Please send to:

Name_____ Ph._____

Address_____

City _____ State _____ Zip _____

The Hawai'i
Tailgate Cookbook: $10.00 x _____ $ _____

Shipping & handling* $ _____

TOTAL ORDER $ _____

❑ Check enclosed, payable to Watermark Publishing

❑ Charge my credit card   ❑ VISA   ❑ MC   ❑ Amex

❑ Discover   ❑ Diner's   ❑ Carte Blanche

Card no._____ Exp. date _____

Signature Required_____

* $4 for one copy, $2 for each additional copy

**Contact us about fundraising opportunities
for your team or organization!**